To Peg,
With best Birthday Wishes
from your Florida cousins —

Shelley F. Mickle

The Kids are Gone; The Dog is Depressed & MOM'S ON THE LOOSE

SHELLEY FRASER MICKLE

ILLUSTRATIONS BY JOHN POTTER

The Alachua Press, Inc.

The Kids are Gone; The Dog is Depressed & Mom's on the Loose

The Alachua Press, Inc. Book

International Standard Book Number 0-9672788-1-3

Library of Congress Catalog Card Number: 00-101312

Design by Susan Grantham
Cover Illustration by John Potter

For information address The Alachua Press, Inc.

513 East University Avenue
Gainesville, FL 32601
352-378-2280

The Alachua Press, Inc. produces historical and popular titles that reflect a wide range of issues concerning the historical development of the region culturally, politically and environmentally.

Printed in the United States of America

Contents

Author's Note

Moving is never easy. Especially from one part of life to the next.

In fact, when I moved to Florida in 1979, I assumed I'd be surrounded by flamingos, snakes, and people with their clothes half off. Nervously, I hunted up my yellow velvet hot pants — the ones my husband gave me in 1969 for our second anniversary.

That was the year a man walked on the moon. It was also the year I had the guts and shape to walk around in hot pants. But ten years later, in 1979, men were going other places than the moon; and I knew I was way past hot pants.

I had more than what-to-wear reservations about living in Florida though. I just didn't know that I could ever call it home. I had lived in too many places where hills and seasonal changes brushed the landscape with a paint box of colors, and where bugs and tulip bulbs went dormant in the winter and knew better than to raise their heads for at least three months out of the year. I even had enough memories of living in places where it snowed that occasionally I dreamed about it. (And I don't think that has a darn thing to do with Freud.)

So I moved in July with my little family — a husband, two children at the ages of nearly three and six — into my little Florida house that was set low against the earth like a dog hunkering down in the heat.

In the fall, I signed up to be a homeroom mother, and I stayed one for the next twelve years. I planted camellias and azaleas and Confederate jasmine in my yard. And I began to think that one of the most wonderful things I had ever heard was a whole slew of bullfrogs croaking throughout the night after a big rain, a rain which Tilly, a long-time and dyed-in-the-wool Floridian, taught me was called a frog-strangler. Yes, there were a lot of frog-strangler rains that first summer.

And when my daughter at the age of eight spent a year taking horseback riding lessons, I found, after driving her out to where it was okay for horses to be kept, a whole network of sand-bottomed roads, some of which were, no doubt, old carriage roadbeds. Sand was on the shoulders a foot deep. Oak trees as tall as buildings arched a lacy canopy of shade across them. And vines looped among the limbs as thick as jungle snakes. But what was strange was that all of that, in one small way or another, echoed the place where I had grown up, and loved best. It was a little cotton town in Arkansas where I had been given the first ideas of who I was. And now, here in my new home, I was feeling that same sense of being anchored, of being okay, of being in place.

So twenty years later I can say without reservation:

1.   Snow is best kept as memories.
2.   Christmas with the air conditioner on is still Christmas. Sometimes better.
3.   Raising children is the funniest thing I have ever done.

And when it's over and they move out, you find you are the vessel holding together the memories of what went into those souls.

That's no small potatoes.

Souls never are.

SHELLEY FRASER MICKLE

Acknowledgments

I owe a special thank you to Kevin Allen at WUFT, who over all these years has taped my essays; and when he first realized this accent of mine has only one gear, very graciously said, "Well, we'll just give you an extra ten seconds."

To my family — Parker, Blake and Paul, who, whenever I have said, "Today I wrote a little essay that had a little bit of you in it — do you mind?" have always replied, "I don't think so."

And to my listeners, who have never failed to stop me in an aisle at the grocery store, or who have come up to me at a gas pump when I was figuring out how to work the darn thing, and asked, "When am I going to be able to read that one about the dog?"

Most of these essays have been read in the same, or similar version, on Florida Public Radio.

Names have been changed to protect the innocent, the shy, or those who would more than likely get their noses out of joint.

Blue Dog

My dog is depressed. She lies under the grand piano with her tobacco-juice eyes closed. Won't even get up when I open a package of wieners, dragging out the tearing of the plastic wrap until all the crackling I am making sounds as if I am setting a fire. But there is no fire in her, not even to get up and investigate. When I hold the wieners in front of a fan to blow the smell toward her — nope — she just lies there, flat, like a rug or an Egyptian sphinx.

What started all of this was when my last child got his driver's license. No more carpools. My dog and I have been taken off the streets. We are home everyday now from two to six. For a while we watched Oprah, and then we'd go out and dig in the dirt around my house.

But my dog doesn't much care about Oprah, and not much more about the dirt. Giving up my carpooling has saddened her.

All those years she went with me to drop the kids off — first in the morning early, when I didn't look good or feel sweet — she'd sit in the back seat of my station wagon and fog up the windows while snapping her teeth. She'd terrify the drivers in the next lane so we could jockey in position to beat the bell. At 2:00 P.M. she'd wait by the back door to go again to pick the kids up. Just the sound of my taking the car keys out of my purse could make her do a tap dance like she had hot feet on the kitchen floor.

From the back seat of my station wagon, she'd hang her head out of the window and let her tongue trail. She is a big mean-looking dog, the kind that men in pick-up trucks with rifles in their back windows admire at red lights. It's not uncommon to have them roll down their windows and get her riled up by making faces at her and then call out to me, "Nice dog, lady."

She's gone to piano lessons and waited at the curb; she likes country music on the radio. She's gone to and come back from soccer practices, Halloween carnivals, and Boy Scout meetings.

Now that she's taken up her down-in-the-mouth spot under the grand piano, I am tempted to pick up the car keys and jiggle them, just to see if she is all right. But that seems cruel. So I have started wrapping the keys in a paper towel so they can be picked up in silence. Because there is nowhere that I go now that I do not park, get out, and stay awhile.

It's a sad event — to just up and change a dog's life with no good warning. She had no way to know that those little kids who played with her as a puppy would one day get cars of their own. Then go on, grow up, and move all the way out.

Yesterday, I felt so sorry for her that I picked up the keys and let her do her hot pepper dance, then headed on out to the car. We've traded in the station wagon. We have a sedan now. And I let her sit beside me in the front seat. As we drove out of the driveway, her big hairy head came on over and rested on my arm near the gear shift.

We made a loop out to the soccer field, then to the piano teacher's where we parked by the curb and listened to the radio. Then we spun on out to the school, even though it was closed. On the way home, I drove her through Burger King and ordered her a Whopper, all the way, but told them to hold the pickles and onions.

Next Sunday I plan to drive her around again. It seems the only decent thing to do for a blue dog.

A Snake Story

I have this thing about snakes. I just have to go on and admit it. I don't like them. Don't care to spend one minute longer with them than I have to. And after I moved into my Florida house, I just assumed my yard would be crawling with them.

Personally I like to have somebody else handle my snake business. But I figured if I were home alone and ran into one, I at least ought to be prepared. I bought myself a hoe. I hung it up in the garage, its new edge bright and gleaming. I doubted I'd ever have the guts to kill a snake with it, but it gave me a sense of calm all the same.

One day when I was vacuuming the family room, a dark spotted snake came across my patio, lifted himself up, spread his neck like a cobra and looked in at me. I dropped my vacuum and ran to the garage to get my hoe.

When I got around to the patio, he was headed for a flower pot. He wasn't very long, but he was fat. And to bolster my fighting spirit, I yelled out a few karate yells. I wanted to let him know that I meant business. He sat up behind the flower pot and hissed at me. I twirled my hoe over my head and let out one long yell to get me revved up enough to bring the hoe down onto his fat head. Just as I was about to, he lay down, rolled over, stuck out his tongue and closed his eyes. This was the first time I had ever succeeded in scaring anything to death.

I bent closer. I leaned over, getting a good look. Then I turned around to go back into my house to drink a little champagne to celebrate my ferociousness. And to calm my nerves.

Sitting there in my family room, I began to think about how some people take joy in wearing snake-skin belts, or boots, and I was beginning to wonder how my own snake now would look around my waist or on my feet. Maybe I'd even start a new trend and design snake-skin barrettes. As I looked out onto the patio to consider how he'd look on me, he sat up, glanced around and slithered off across the yard into the woods.

The next day I told this snake story to the man who sprays my house for bugs. He laughed. "Oh that's just a hog-nose snake," he said. "You can't even get him to bite. His only defense is playing tricks. Acts like every bad snake there is, and if that don't work, he plays dead. Guess he figures nobody wants a dead snake."

I didn't add that personally that's the way I like them best.

Now, I'm not going to say that I've finally met a snake I like. But there is something rather endearing about one that will act like a cobra, hiss like a cat, roll over and play dead, then get up and go on about his business, not to mention get a kick out of watching some-one vacuum. That is, I guess, a snake after my own heart.

Hair

Today I was going out the door to get my hair fixed. I had a weekend guest staying at my house, and she asked me, "Does your hairdresser know everything about you?"

Well, I guess he does. But it is not necessarily because of anything I have told him.

It's a known fact that hair doesn't lie. Oh, you can get it to. Like it can be dyed to cover up the years. And it can be curled up into a spiffy 'do' to hide a down-in-the-mouth mood. But the bottom line is that any thing that happens to you can show up in your hair. I've read that some laboratory somewhere can take the last few inches of a person's hair and find out all sorts of things, such as that they are taking a medicine or using drugs.

Back when I was young, hair could state what side of the Vietnam War you were on. Advertisements said hair was not only a social problem, it was a drain problem. At twenty-two, my goal was to grow my hair long enough to sit on. I don't know why. Surely that would not have been comfortable. I think I just wanted to tick my mother off.

But now I get it trimmed religiously. I am working, too, to keep the gray where I want it to be, in a well-planned attack to look dignified.

My mother raised me to call the place where we went to get our hair fixed a beauty parlor. But now it makes more sense to call it the hairdresser's, since that is what we do, dress our hair to get it to say what we want it to.

When I sit in that whirly chair and get pumped up to chest-height on the hairdresser, I look down at the inches he trims off. This week, it's the hair I wore when I burned last Tuesday's spaghetti and ran over the edge of the driveway and killed a bush. It's also the hair I wore to my daughter's college graduation and to the last baseball game that my son played.

As the shampoo girl sweeps all of it up into a dustpan, I imagine reaching for it, holding it for a second, and then carefully tucking all of it inside my head.

This Thing
Called Memory

I was in the grocery store the other day, going up and down the aisles as I usually do, putting into my cart a little of this, and a little of that, for I never use a grocery list.

Nope, making up a grocery list is just way too organized for me. I prefer strolling by all the items on the shelves and letting the sight of each one of them jog my memory into realizing that I either need it, or I don't. And of course, too, this leaves a good bit of room for that impulse buy, like the two cartons of macadamia nuts I brought home last week because it was a special of the day — buy one and get one free — the idea of which got me so excited, I forgot I'm allergic to macadamia nuts. Now, I guess, I'm going to have to feed them to the dog.

But anyway, it was right after I bought those nuts that I swung around Aisle Two and ran into a man who instantly knew me. He reached open his arms and swept me up into them while halfway singing with joy, "Why, just looky here who I've found! I'm so glad to see you!" I looked into his face and hugged him back and said that I was so really glad to see him, too. And then I waited for his name to come to me.

Now it always takes me a little bit of time to sort out all the faces and names that I have known over the last twenty years. In fact, I used to roll my son in diapers through the same grocery store every week, and I have never gone there since that I do not see someone with whom I have been acquainted, either in my kids' school, through my husband's work, from my own classes that I teach, or just by being in the same neighborhood. Living in a small city like ours, where you can almost always bump into someone you know, is enough to make me take a bath and comb my hair before I head off to the grocery store. I just assumed I knew the man who was swallowing me in a bear hug.

His face was so full of joy in seeing me that I was sure we had once been very special to each other. I was wondering if he could be my son's second grade teacher who so warmly reassured me that, no, I had not ruined my son by teaching him how to play craps because it was the best way I knew for him to practice the addition tables. Or, he could be the man who promised not to tell anybody when he found me at a mother-son picnic beating the fishing worms to death because I couldn't stand to put them on the hooks wiggling.

But now, a woman, who was apparently this man's wife, was touching me on my arm and apologizing. "He thinks he knows you," she whispered, and then she took him by the hand and coaxed him away, glancing back at me with the embarrassment of one who cares for someone whose memory has been misaligned by a disease that is usually accompanied by age. I felt sorry that she was embarrassed, for I can't remember when I have been the object of such a joyful greeting. My face must have jiggled loose someone very special in his past. And I was more than happy to be to him whoever he wanted me to be. Besides, my own memories were making up parts for him in my life, too.

It is said that God gave us memory so that we might have roses in December. And Tennessee Williams once wrote that in memory everything seems to happen to music.

Well, last week in the grocery store I had one of my finest hours. I was a rose dancing in a memory.

Devils

All my life I've been fascinated with the idea of eternal damnation. It stems from the time when I was five years old, and my grandmother told me that if I didn't stop telling fibs and stealing nickels from her purse, I was going to end up *Down There*. After which she would point straight to the floor with her second finger which was manicured in a devilish red. Not even lying spread eagle and buck naked on a block of ice would cool me off, she said. (My grandmother always had a knack for graphic descriptions.) So I gave up lying and stealing, though now I am haunted with the ideas of what made me go straight.

I grew up thinking that when you got eternally damned, you were sent somewhere under the earth where everything was red — the devils, the flames, the rivers and trees, even the roads, because of course everything was on fire. And the only thing that was a little different was the brimstone, which no doubt was white with heat and you were poked with a pitchfork to be made to walk barefoot over it, back and forth going nowhere, just on and on forever. I figured once you got used to the pain, if you ever did, boredom would get you next.

When I became a teenager, the idea that maybe boredom wouldn't necessarily be a part of eternal damnation came to me with clarity. Because I knew a lot of people who were flirting with what my grandmother had led me to believe would get anybody sent *Down There*, and they were definitely fun to have at a party. If by a fluke I did end up *Down There,* and they were already there or fell in after, it couldn't be all bad I decided. The only thing I thought I couldn't handle would be if I were assigned to be a roommate with a certain few of them. That's when my ideas of eternal damnation changed.

It has become very clear to me in my adulthood that being *Down There* is nothing more than a long line of rooms, really small rooms with high walls and smooth floors, and no one enters one alone. You are put in with something or someone who is chosen for you. Yes, eternal damnation is individualized; I'm sure of it. I've asked some of my friends about it, and they are quick to tell me that I am right.

My neighbor says that if she were eternally damned she would be shut into a room with her dog sucking his fleas. And another friend has told me that if he ends up *Down There*, he will be shut up with Ross Perot and an unlimited supply of poster board and magic markers. As for me, well, personally the last place I'd like to be is in a room with a washing machine and a teenager's laundry.

Of course that's no longer a threat now. But maybe it's just as well. I think it's kind of neat to keep the Devil guessing.

The Piano

When my children were home with me and I was raising them, I had an odd form of torture. I came up with it because it was the only thing I knew I could stick with. I mean, I'm not one who is big on discipline myself. I've been known to eat a whole cake at one sitting, and I can go for days without emptying the garbage. So I had to invent something that would teach my children stick-to-itiveness and the joy of completion and all those other things that make a person fine and upstanding. I signed them up for piano lessons.

I made them memorize that old saying, "Practice makes perfect." Then we pretty much proved it is a lie. I eventually bought a grand piano so it would look like we were really serious. Then I made my kids get up a half hour earlier before school to sit at the piano bench and plunk at the keys, so maybe their teacher would be convinced they had put in the required amount of practice time. Of course I would feed them first, and they would be mostly dressed, but they had to sit there until it was time for the car pool or the school bus.

We kept it up for seven long years. All the while, the dog would lie under the piano and watch my children's feet going up and down on the pedals, which most often they did in sock feet.

My son got really good on that song, "Great Balls of Fire." And whenever he played the chorus, the dog would sit up and howl. Sometimes, she got almost as excited as Jerry Lee Lewis.

The piano is quiet now. No one plays it much anymore. Occasionally one of the cats walks across the keys as if it is trying on shoes. But whenever I look at that piano or think about dusting it, I remember how I always thought it could beautifully illustrate what sounds like a Bible Verse: "And so it was that the right hand did not know what the left hand doeth."

The hands are attached to two fine upstanding people, though. And that piano — well, it's going to be worth a bundle as an antique.

Sayings

I grew up saying all sorts of things when I didn't really know what in the world they meant; like saying "what in the world" when I am really perplexed. I know that saying it was handed down to me by people in my family and in my southern culture, but I don't have a cotton picking idea why I yell out "What in the world am I doing?" when I drive off the wrong exit on I-75. Because where else am I when all these perplexing things happen, but in the world? Indeed, where else could anything happen but on the planet that I am currently inhabiting? But still, I go right on saying things like "What in the world am I doing here?"

I don't have a cotton-picking idea, either, why I say "cotton picking idea" when my mind is blank. I haven't picked cotton in more than forty years, and it wasn't my idea to pick it in the first place. When I am really stunned and yell out "For Crying Out Loud!" I know that all logic has left my brain, because where else is the best place to cry but out loud, since everybody knows that whimpering and keeping a stiff upper lip can lead to ulcers and heart trouble?

In the summer when I was little, I used to hear in reference to my face that I had more freckles than you could shake a stick at. Now that carries the notion of a great quantity, and I think it's kind of neat. But it also carries for me the sense of dealing with snakes, since I assume the people who handed that saying down to me had shaken sticks at a whole lot of critters and especially snakes to get them to hightail it out of their yards.

"Hightail it", of course, comes from cowboys describing how horses head off with their tails high when they are going somewhere lickety-split. And lickety-split says it all, because there's no way you can say it without your tongue doing exactly what it says.

Oh, there's no doubt about it, I am armed with a stunning array of exclamations that fly out of my mouth with no thought or logic at all but that define the situation to a T.

There are times when I know that I have appeared as dumb as a doornail, and yet I think a doornail is pretty nifty since it's holding together part of a door. But then there are times, too, that I've come off as smart as a whip; and yet I've never known a whip to do calculus or much of anything if it wasn't attached to the arm of someone.

My grandmother used to say I was, "slow as molasses," and whenever she served me pancakes and I poured on my own syrup, I knew what she meant. But then, mornings aren't my thing, and if the molasses takes a good ten minutes getting out of its bottle, that only gives me a little extra time to wake up.

My favorite saying is when someone wants to get across a real important fact, and they start out by telling you that it goes without saying, and then they go right on and say it.

So, it goes without saying that I really don't think I could get through a day now without my sayings. I've got one to fit almost every situation. When they don't make sense that often seems appropriate, too, such as an hour ago when my daughter called and said she'd just had the transmission fall all the way out of her car. "Oh, for Pete's sake!" I said. And I don't even have a cotton pickin' idea who Pete is.

Watermelon

My grandmother added a footnote to that saying that you can tell a whole lot about a person by his shoes. She said you can tell a whole lot more by the way a person eats watermelon.

The first time I ate one, I was four. At least that's the first time I remember my father stopping at a roadside stand and taking me with him to buy one. He bent down toward the ground where a whole army of melons was laid out, and he began thumping them, his fingers curled like a good door spring slamming against the green rind. I never could catch onto the sound he was looking for, even though he tried to tell me. Yet when he came upon it, he seemed to instantly know.

The melons all sounded alike to me, something like the brass section of a band tuning up, their deep notes all tangled together. But my father, after thumping on a half dozen for a good long while, could sort out the baritones from the tubas, the French horns from the trumpets, and roll onto the back seat of the car a watermelon in its eating prime.

Back home we'd put newspapers all over the top of the picnic table out in the backyard, and my father would take a big butcher knife and cut through our chosen melon with great ceremony. He was convinced that eating wedges of watermelon was a waste, that no one really got down to the last little bit because they wouldn't give up the use of their fork, which really wasn't very good at separating the fruit from the rind in the first place. He insisted instead on slicing the melon into two-inch disks which he then bisected so that when we bit into our pieces, we made a half-moon frame for our faces as we ate clear down to the rind. And all of this without the benefit of a fork or a plate or a napkin, which really weren't necessary since we just leaned over and let the seeds and juice drip onto the grass.

Those seeds. That was a matter of great discussion. How you disposed of them revealed exactly where you were in your personality development — swallow them, spit them, daintily pick them out with a fork or less daintily with a finger. My father was a spitter. He'd take a couple of bites of melon, then inside his mouth separate the seeds from the fruit and launch the seeds onto the ground like someone versed in the ways of handling chewing tobacco.

For a while I was a swallower; I just didn't have the patience to separate the seeds from the fruit. But I changed when my brother told me that one of those little seeds was going to take root in my stomach and pretty soon I would have a whole watermelon vine crawling inside me and coming out just wherever it could. So for the rest of my childhood, I became a spitter like my father.

When I turned thirteen, I started tunneling into the watermelon with my finger so I could torpedo the seeds out, which also meant that I had to take up the use of a plate since I had to have something to lean the melon against to get some leverage on it. Most of those dern pesky little seeds were way down in there, and I had to poke a good bit.

By the time I had graduated from college, I finally broke down and took up the use of a fork. I would pick the seeds out of each section of melon with the fork tines, set the seeds on the side of my plate, then cut the melon and stick it with the fork and lift it to my mouth. I usually even followed that up with a napkin.

But there is something I have never ever been able to give up, and it doesn't matter where I am — in a grocery store, a roadside stand, a restaurant or a country club, just anywhere where a melon is on display: I thump it. I give the thick green rind a good pop, and then lean close, pretending that I can tell whenever I come upon a tuba or a French horn.

And as for those watermelons advertised as seedless? Well, the idea is nice, but personally I wouldn't have one in my house. In fact, the minute my children feel a little serious about someone they're dating, I'm going to bring out a watermelon and give them the old personality test.

Hearts

My first valentine was a red hot — not in a package but single and sticky, as though whoever had decided to give it to me had held it a long while. I was seven and in the second grade, and it sat on the top of my desk after recess like an ink dot.

All afternoon when the teacher wasn't looking, I kept whirling around hoping to meet the eyes of my admirer. He never did have the courage to come forward, but a single red hot was enough to convince me that I was the object of someone's desire.

It was special, being liked by someone who was not my mother or father or any other kin. This is something the world owes you, I think: to be prized for who you are and by someone who is not related and therefore is not obligated to value you.

My admirer finally revealed himself to me late that spring. When the teacher was out of the room, Calvin Muldoon jumped on me from behind, wrestled me to the floor and tickled me until I was nearly incontinent, and all the while he was singing, "Hey Good Lookin, What You Got Cookin?"

Frankly I wish he'd just left things at the level of one red hot. I didn't feel the same way about him that he did about me. I couldn't bear to tell him that, but even worse was that the charm of the mystery was gone.

The way I handled things then was that the next day I pushed him out of the swing at recess, and, when he thought this was a sign of my affection, I told him his nose was dripping and he couldn't come over to my house ever again.

This mean deed got back at me on Valentine's Day when I was in tenth grade. It was so imperative to have someone hot on you that I bought my own large box of chocolates. I put them in my locker at school as though someone had planted them there. It was the only way I could get the other girls to think highly of me, since by then we all valued each other by the measure of which boy valued us.

Now I'm thinking of taking a different tact on Valentine's. I'm tempted to indiscriminately send cards to people I pick out of the phone book whom I don't even know. I'll sign them. They won't know me either. But I figure that if I don't make them think they are losing their minds, I will at least spark in them a sense of wonder.

Maybe it's mean — to plant a mystery this way and not to ever follow it up. But my belief is that hearts are delicate things, prone to disease and hairline cracks. They are easily fed by imagination, though. And there's nothing quite like being admired by someone for no other reason than that you exist, and have a name.

Grandma's Organ

I've finally learned how to pull out all the stops. I know that when I was growing up, I threatened to do it a good many times. Like when I was running a bicycle race with my brother, and I'd be trailing about a good half mile behind. Then as the backstretch came into view, I'd yell out to him that he better watch out because I was pulling out all the stops. I'd whiz past him then and let him eat my dust. But I never did. It just never happened.

All my life, it seems to have gone on like this. No matter how many times and over how many things I have threatened to pull out all my stops, nothing much has ever come about. Even my children—on whom clearly I had a jump, since I could talk before they could and for a long while was bigger than — just blew me off. In fact, from almost the moment they were born, I have been warning them that I was going to pull out all the stops over one thing or another. But about all I have ever gotten is one second of their attention.

Now, though, I have discovered my grandmother's organ. I don't mean a body part. I'm talking about the church organ she was bequeathed from her country Methodist church back in 1953. That's when the church got a modern organ that was hooked up to metal pipes that could blow the stained glass out of the windows. But the one I'm talking about is the one that the church used probably through most of the late 1800s, the one you have to pump to give it the air to blow out the notes. And now I have it. It is right there in my living room.

All across its keys are little black knobs that are — miracle of miracles — called the stops. These stops have words written on them in the most beautiful old script, labeling the first one the *Treble Coupler*, and the next one the *Box Angelica, 8 ft.* Then the *Melodia, 8 ft.*, followed by the *Dulcet Treble, 8 ft.*, then the *Box Humana*. The one near the middle is called the *Principal*, then right there above where your left hand would be is the *Violina 4 ft.*, then the *Viola 4 ft.*, then the *Bass Coupler*, and finally, the *Sub Bass 16 ft.* When you pull out these stops, the notes you are playing make a whole different sound, and of course underneath your feet are pumping like crazy. But if you really want to get attention, you pull out the stop named *Bass Coupler* so that when you push down one key, another one, a whole octave lower, is coupled with it, so it seems you are playing with four hands. And if you really want to blow off the roof, you pull out the big enchilada, the *Sub Bass 16 ft.*, and play *The Battle Hymn of the Republic*.

Always in the past during holiday seasons, I have played a lot of sweet hymns on my grandmother's organ. And whenever I do, my family and friends tend to come quietly into the room and stand around behind me and sing. But I've decided that this year, I'm going to stop being a liar. When they all come to stand around me, I'm going to open the hymn book to *The Battle Hymn of the Republic*, pull out all the stops and blow everybody out of the room.

Thank goodness for my grandmother's organ.

Willie Mae

When I was growing up in Arkansas in the early fifties, my grandmother on my father's side told me that I must not ever count money in front of an open window. She also said that if a man tried to sway me with flattery, I should slap him in the face. I guess both of these things were appropriate to know for someone like her who was born in 1886.

She also had a woman who came to work at her house several times a week. She was black, and her name was Willie Mae. You see, my grandmother had been in a buggy accident in 1911. She'd been sitting in the buggy alone when a pig ran up under the horse, and it spooked, took off, and the buggy crashed against a tree. My grandmother was severely handicapped, and really did need a lot of daily help. But it was when my grandmother tried to teach me how I should act around Willie Mae that I decided my grandmother had a screw loose. For I was taught that Willie Mae was never to come to the front door. She was never to sit down in the kitchen and eat with me. In fact, she was never to sit down in any room with me at any time. And if she was to be the one to take me to the Saturday afternoon movie at the Ritz, she was to sit in the balcony while I sat downstairs with the other white people.

None of this made sense to me, and I let my grandmother know about it. Oh, but it was the way things were supposed to be, she told me.

And then she brought out her Bible and read it. She read Genesis 9:18-27 about Noah running a vineyard and one day getting drunk and falling asleep naked. His son Ham saw him and told his brother. And when Noah woke up, he was so furious in his embarrassment that he put a curse on Ham's son, Canaan, saying all the children of Canaan and his children's children would be slaves forever. According to my grandmother, this was the family line in the Bible that Willie Mae was descended from. And that was proof that she was supposed to work for us and stay in her place; and if she didn't like it, she was supposed to at least not talk about it.

Later when I got the Bible down and read those pages by myself, I found out that Noah didn't have Ham until he was five hundred years old. No doubt he was burned out from childraising, and his sons had driven him to drink on the day he had waked up cursing. And there's nothing said anywhere about Ham or his son Canaan being black, yellow, or any other thing. That's when I learned about the power of interpretation. Words lifted off the page can be made to mean anything.

Eventually, I turned this experience into fiction while I was writing my first novel, *The Queen of October*. But the whole time I was living it, it became the root of a great confusion that took me a long while to sort out. For it is never easy to come to know that you can still love someone while at the same time you detest their beliefs.

Once when I was sick and in the hospital, Willie Mae wrote me a long letter, all of it backwards. She included instructions to hold it up to a mirror to read it. It took me most of a delightful afternoon to unravel, like magic, what she was writing to me. She gave me gifts at Christmas and for my high school graduation. Yes, Willie Mae became more to me than the woman who worked for my grandmother. She became part of my own personal history.

She is in her sixties now. She has served on the town council in that same little cotton town where I grew up. She is prominent in state politics, and she is a grandmother now, herself. She writes a newspaper column every week; and on occasion, she still writes to me. She is living proof of how we have changed.

But what I wonder is, if our places had been reversed — if I had been in her grandmother's house as she had been in mine, would I have been as good, as forgiving, as loyal, as compassionate? I tend to doubt it. But I can say this: Black history month is more than a month of histories. All of our stories should be rewritten to include how we have existed together truthfully, and less than truthfully, for all of this time. For knowing how we never want to be again is as valuable as seeing how we never like to admit we were.

Nickel Words

When I was a year old, my father took a job helping to build a power plant in Pennsylvania. We all moved up there — my father, my mother, my brother and I, all the way from Arkansas to Pennsylvania — which meant that when my brother started the first grade he came home everyday talking like a northerner. My parents thought that was cute. But no one thought it was cuter than my Great Uncle Bubba back in Tennessee.

The idea that southerners have people in their family called Bubba has become a cliché now, and probably half the time people don't believe it anyway. But my great uncle Bubba was born in 1895, the last child after a line of eight girls who all called him Little Brother, which eventually got shortened to Little Bubba. By the time he was my great uncle, he resembled Santa Claus in a seersucker suit, and the word "little" no longer applied.

When we all went home for a family reunion, what tickled Uncle Bubba the most was not just my brother talking but me. For when I had left the South, I couldn't say anything except baby sounds. And now that I was back visiting as a sassy three-year-old, every word out of my mouth was short, clipped, and wrapped in what my uncle called a Yankee brogue. It seems that like all the viruses and germs that my brother had brought home from school, I had also picked up from him his new and peculiar way of saying things. So Uncle Bubba took my brother and me out onto the porch and entertained our relatives by giving us a nickel for every sentence we said. "Just listen to those little Yankee words!" he exclaimed.

It was a wonderful thing to get paid for just talking. And for the next three years I could rely on my Great Uncle Bubba to make me one of the richest kids in Pennsylvania. But then, when the power plant was built and my parents were too homesick to move to where the next one was going to be, we headed back to Arkansas, and I entered the first grade. At the next family reunion, Uncle Bubba took me out onto the porch and asked me, "And so, what's your favorite food?" No doubt I said something sassy like "Cotton candy," sounding like I sound now, and his face fell. He gave me the nickel anyway, then sent me off to play with my cousins. Apparently my Yankee accent had been soaked away in the brine of twenty other first graders who'd spent their whole lives in Arkansas. I think Uncle Bubba knew my Yankee accent was temporary. He knew we would move back. I think that's why he paid me in the first place. For I know that surely he wouldn't have liked me if I were a full-grown Yankee woman.

In 1968, when I was married, I moved North again. No one paid me nickels for talking, but I sensed some people might have paid me to keep quiet. By the winter of my second year there, I had all the right equipment to pass as a native: a long wool coat, fur-lined boots, and a Volvo. Any car built in Sweden would surely know how to get around in snow. But every time a snow storm was predicted, I felt a twinge of hysteria.

One day in the first hour of a large storm, I flew out of the house in a blur of snowflakes to hurry to the grocery store. When I turned onto the main road, I slid into the median. My Volvo had its whole hood stuck into a snowbank as white as ginned cotton, and as I was getting out, two people were running toward me. "Are you all right?" one was yelling. And the other asked, "How'd this happen?"

"Goodness!" I said. "I guess I just put the brakes on too fast. I'm not used to driving in this stuff."

As soon as they heard me talk, they both stood back. One of them said, "Well, that explains it," and then the other one added, "No wonder."

I lived in the Northeast for nearly a decade. And while I was up there, I began to think of my accent in the same way that some people seemed to — as a badge of stupidity. I worked hard to get rid of it. But I couldn't.

What jolted me back into some sense of balance were cocktail parties. All that time spent on your feet eating tiny food and drinking drinks — a person's soul can come unwrapped. And in 1968, a lot of people were upset about what the country was doing and about the changes that were happening. More than once, when someone heard my accent, he or she would come up to me and say something like, "Doesn't all this civil rights stuff make you sick? Isn't it going to be awful with blacks and whites mixing everywhere?"

Now my question is this — if my accent signaled that I might be stupid, or at least close, and yet they assumed we both held the same view, what does that say about the view?

It never has made any sense to me. In a roundabout way, I think my Great Uncle Bubba taught me that. Not because he believed that skin color doesn't matter, because he believed that it did. But because he was willing to pay me to talk differently.

I can still see us: him and me, sitting on the porch, the shiny nickel balanced on the end of his wide thumb, his white hair thick and cut to about the length of a toothpick. "Say it again," he would say. Sure, in some ways he was making fun of me. But in my way of thinking, he was celebrating what he found in me that was different from him.

I'm glad he didn't regard it as a bargain.

Tin Cans

The world is changing so fast that keeping up could worry me to death. But I've decided not to let it. I know that sooner or later I'm going to have to pull onto the information highway. But when I do I plan to have my rearview mirrors shined up, so I can easily remember when talking into a tin can, with a string strung out of the bottom of it, could give me a thrill.

The day my brother and I decided to make homemade walkie-talkies, I was nine, and it was 1953. Ordinarily we didn't have much to say to each other, and what we did say wasn't always nice. But when we got on our tin cans, things between us changed. He would get on one side of the yard behind a tree like Sergeant Joe Friday, and I'd get on the other, hunkered down near a bush like his good-natured side kick. And the string that we'd anchored by a knot in the bottom of our tin cans would be pulled tight between us.

"Can you hear me?" he'd say.

"Pretty good," I'd say back, talking into my tin can, and then I'd put it to my ear.

"Well, what's going on over there?" he'd ask.

"Not much," I'd report, and then say, "There's just a bird right over my head in this bush."

"What's he doing?" my brother wanted to know.

And I'd tell him, "Just sitting there," then add to myself, "Thank the Lord." Because I knew that if that bird decided to drop something onto my head, my brother would have that fact spread all over the neighborhood faster than walkie-talkie string could take it.

"Here comes Mom to hang out the laundry," he'd report.

"What's she got on?" I'd ask.

When my brother and I had finished talking, I think we'd learned more about each other and our family through those tin cans than we did without them.

So now when I see someone on a cellular phone, either in a restaurant or in a car beside me, I like to think the best – that they're actually talking to someone they ordinarily wouldn't. And this must be true for surfing the internet and getting on the world wide web, too. At least the names they're called, "net" and "web," are leading us to believe that we are all being tied up together and becoming closer.

But I know I've gone at least three whole months talking to someone's answering machine, leaving messages on it which they returned on mine. And just like my brother's tin can conversations, these carry a whole different personality than what I'd get if I sat down across from that person where the expressions in his face and the gestures of his hands would tell me how he really thought and felt.

There's no doubt about it, all these electronic communications are cleaning us up, putting us on our best behavior, which is nice. But I know, too, that whenever my mother made me put on my best behavior, most of the time it meant I had to lie. On my best behavior I didn't blow air through a straw to bubble up my drink, or pull my legs up under me in the church pew so I could really get comfortable through a long sermon, or tell Aunt Ollie that her house smelled like sauerkraut and I couldn't wait to go home.

These menus now that the phones are putting us on — Press one, if you want such and such, and two if want this or that—they're letting us order communications as we would a Big Mac or a hot fudge sundae. I know they are quick and efficient, and they put us all on our best behavior. But sometimes just for old times' sake, I wait for that last choice in the menu which is usually there: "If you're on a rotary phone, stay on the line and someone will answer."

Usually I really am on my old rotary phone, which I am keeping for sentimental reasons. But then other times, when I am on my quick dial and am lying, it's just that I'm a little hungry for the sound of another unrecorded voice.

The Price of Silver

In 1949 when I was five years old, I could make the sound of a galloping horse on the roof of my mouth with my tongue. I could barrel a whole posse down on my mother from the back seat of our car while she was driving me somewhere. And I stampeded my brother out in the backyard whenever I snuck up on him. But what I was really good at was riding homemade stick horses made out of brooms.

That summer, my parents had to go out of town, and my maternal grandmother and her little sister came to our house to baby-sit me and my brother. About twenty minutes after my parents had driven out of our driveway, I turned to my grandmother, looked straight into her face and told her I had to have a new horse. All year, I'd been riding around on this red broom named Big Red, and I'd made him rear up so much on his straw — you see, his front legs were my legs — that I'd worn him slap out.

My grandmother looked back at me. She wasn't a whole lot taller than I was. And my great aunt was even smaller than my grandmother. If they ever needed a job, I thought they were perfect circus material. Both of them wore cotton dresses, with little dots on them, and thick-heeled lace-up shoes. Talcum powder spread up their necks like the sugar on donuts. And they wore stockings even in the hottest of weather, which they rolled up into a thick bunch around a garter just over their knees. Both of them were pillars in their church.

"All right," my grandmother said and went to get her purse. I knew she was desperate to keep me quiet, if not happy. For I think my whole family was a little afraid of me back then. Not only was I passionate about my brooms, but I'd also become a specialist at throwing screaming-mimi fits. Whenever I'd let go with one of these in public, my grandmother was not only ashamed, but also terrified. You see, my grandmother worried all the time that someone in our family was carrying a gene with hereditary insanity on it, and that one day craziness would just pop out and undo everything my family had accomplished for generations. I don't know what accomplishments she was talking about. I couldn't put my finger on one thing outstanding or even out of the ordinary that anyone in my family had ever done, except for maybe my great great grandfather who got shot in the stomach with a cannon ball at the Civil War battle of Shiloh and carried that cannon ball around in his stomach until he died of the flu. But anyway, my grandmother worried all the time that our family would get tarnished by hereditary insanity. And since my screaming-mimi fits made it look like I might be carrying the gene for it, I pretty much got everything I wanted, if I promised not to let go with one in public.

So we started off to the grocery store to get my new broom, which was to be my new horse. We had to walk because neither my grandmother nor her little sister could drive. You see, they were grown women when cars came into their lives, and they never could get the hang of driving them. In fact, whenever they had tried, their knees had shaken so much they'd accidentally turned off the ignition. So they'd just given up and walked to wherever they wanted to go, or else caught a ride with someone who had a car. The store around the corner from my house was the only one we could walk to. We were living in Hot Springs, Arkansas, then, and there were a lot of hills all over; and my grandmother and her little sister were huffing a good bit. All the way there, I kept reminding my grandmother that this was to be my show. "I can pick out any one I want to, right?" I warned her.

"Within reason," she said.

"I'm gonna name it Silver," I told her.

She was panting pretty hard now, and my little great aunt, who was secretly adjusting her girdle through her skirt, was breathing hard too.

When we reached the grocery store, we walked in and headed straight to the back. Brooms were pretty important in those days, and they were displayed all over the walls, nailed up nearly to the ceiling. My grandmother and I both pitched back our necks and let our eyes walk up the walls, while my great aunt stood behind us wiping perspiration off her face with a handkerchief that she kept tucked in her bosom. Then I saw the broom I had to have near the ceiling.

Probably I chose it because I'd heard so many of those fairy tales about a prince riding up on a white horse and saving some pitiful but good-looking girl in some terrible mess she'd gotten herself into that never made much sense to me in the first place. If I couldn't quite buy the idea that the prince was the answer to the girl's trouble, I was all the way sold on what the horse would do for her. No, it wasn't the prince I was interested in back then. It was his horse I wanted.

My grandmother pointed out to the clerk the broom I'd chosen. But the clerk looked back at her and asked, "How about that red one?" He pointed to over the boxes of Tide.

"I already have a red one," I told my grandmother.

My grandmother looked from the clerk to me and back to the clerk. "It's true," she said, "we already have a red one."

"Then what about that blue one?" He pointed. It was just a little higher than the red one. My chosen white one was not only near the ceiling, it was mounted over three other rows of brooms and lots of shelves full of household cleaners and cans of turnip greens and bottles of hot sauce.

My grandmother turned to face me. "You don't really have to have that exact one, do you?"

"Yep," I said.

She looked back at the clerk. "We'd really like that white one, if you don't mind."

I was only five years old and didn't know yet what grown-ups sat on and what they held back, but no doubt that clerk was dying to ask, "What damn difference is it what color your broom is, lady?" But he didn't. I'm sure he was wondering, too, why we were consulting so much about it.

I wanted my grandmother to go on and tell him it was to be MY broom and the color was important because, after all, it was to be a white horse. But she was probably too embarrassed to let anyone outside of our family know what power I had over them. And, too, maybe she was ashamed we were the kind of family who would spend good money to let one of us ride around on a broom. In her mind, it might have made us appear semi-uncouth and a little trashy.

But I do remember a lot of consultation, and then finally that little man got a ladder and placed it against the shelves of laundry powder and climbed up on it.

He knocked down a few boxes of Tide as he took the wooden tip of one broom and stuck it up into the straw of my chosen white one and wiggled it. So the white one got unhooked, and it came crashing down on the floor by us. It landed in front of my nervous little great aunt, and she let out a, "Lord-A-Mercy!" then picked it up and handed it to me.

My grandmother, out of the embarrassment of all the trouble we were causing, bent over and picked up the two knocked-down boxes of Tide and quickly said, "Oh, I just remembered. We need some of this."

I had enough sense of decorum not to hop on Silver until he and the Tide were paid for. But as soon as we were outside on the sidewalk, I got on and galloped a good ways ahead. Then out of a sense of guilt, stirred with some gratitude, I turned around, trotted back to my grandmother and handed her Silver and said, "Y'all can swap off riding him. I 'spec he's real good on these hills."

Maybe my grandmother was afraid I'd have one of those screaming-mimi fits, or maybe she really was affected by the sight of those hills. But anyway, she took my broom, swung her leg over, and galloped Silver nearly all the way home. Then at the bottom of the driveway, she trotted back, handed him over to my little great aunt, who, after she adjusted her girdle, made Silver rear up.

It seems to me we passed around that insanity gene pretty good, that afternoon.

You're Whose?

There's an old saying that I grew up with, and it goes like this. In the East, it's what you know that counts. In the West, it's how you look. And in the South, well, you don't stand a mole's chance in Hell if you aren't related to somebody. And preferably it's somebody who's lived in the exact same place for about a hundred years.

My grandmother made it her business to know who was related to whom in the whole county. To her it was a game. She collected family histories the way I collected bubble gum cards. I couldn't have any kid over after school but that my grandmother didn't sit them down at the kitchen table and grill them about who their parents were and who their grandparents were, and aunts and uncles and so on back until the time of the Big Bang, if she could get it. Of course none of my friends knew much past the names and addresses of their grandparents, but it didn't matter. Because give my grandmother an inch of family history and she could run it all the way back to the Big Bang, which is what she called the Civil War. And if she couldn't, well, the sun didn't set one more time but that she could.

She would sit in the living room with the preacher on one of his afternoon visits, and they'd start talking about one family, and then follow it to another as if they were pulling a thread loose from a sweater. Pretty soon they'd fill up a whole hour of conversation by unraveling that one family, whom they hopped and skipped all over the county. And then they'd start on somebody else in the congregation.

My grandmother may have been the champ at knowing whom you came from, but everybody all over town practiced it. In a cotton town of a couple of thousand people, we were all related by time and proximity. We were joined by the weather we experienced, the failure or success of our crops, the sicknesses we spread and recovered from and could commiserate with each other about. I remember how it was to walk down the crowded sidewalks on Saturdays when all the farmers would come into town for supplies and be stopped by any number of them who asked, "You're whose?" This was shorthand for "Who's your family," or, "Whom do you come from?" And when I told them, they'd usually turn to one of their own kin standing there and say something like, "Oh, heck! we shoulda knowed that. Just look at her grandmother right there in her chin. And those eyes. Lawsamercy! I've seen those eyes on only one other person in this whole town, and that's her daddy."

Yep, there was comfort in knowing families were going on and on, and it was scary, too. Because you learned at an early age you were branded by your chin and your eyes, or some other body part that could give you away.

My fondest memory is of galloping my stick horse down the back alley to the drug store and hitching ol' Silver up to a light pole and going in for a whole package of bubble gum or one long yellow pencil whose eraser smelled like fresh sawn wood and was as flat as new pavement. "Charge it," I'd say, and the soda jerk would look up at me and know right off by my chin and my nose whom to send the bill to.

My friend Edalu got a speeding ticket when she was in high school. She admits she was asking for it, riding around in a convertible sports car with the top down and her hair flying out like some flag. The only thing was, she was sure she wasn't speeding; she just looked like someone who would. In fact, she was going turtle slow to be sure all the boys at football practice could get a good look at her. So she went to court to fight the charge.

She stood up in front the judge, and he looked straight at her and asked, "You're whose?" When she told him, then added she hadn't been speeding a bit, he asked, "Got any proof?"

"Only my word, sir," she replied, after which he banged his gavel down hard and announced, "That's enough for me."

Of course, neither of them mentioned that at the time he was dating her aunt.

I'll admit anonymity is nice: getting lost in a crowd, moving some place where everybody else is on the move, too. You can go to the grocery store with your hair uncombed and in need of a bath. But it's kind of sad, too, when nobody makes you run and hide behind a mound of potatoes. Or comes to hunt you out and ask, "You're whose?"

Long Distance Christmas

When I was a child, a few days before Christmas Eve, my grandmother would call my parents in Arkansas two hours away from her, and say, "Saturday. Pecans. Fruitcake. And Mentholatum." Then hang up. We knew then when to go meet her bus for her holiday visit, that she was bringing a sack of pecans and a fruitcake, and that she had a cold.

You see, all her life my grandmother was afraid of the telephone. After all, she was a grown woman when the first one came into her house. For as long as she lived, she believed that whenever she was talking on one, at any given moment the telephone mouthpiece could spit a shock of electricity straight at her. Just in case this happened, and the words she said might be her last, she always kept her conversations short, to the point, and intentionally sweet.

She'd get off the Greyhound bus for her Christmas visit in a bright red dress with her hair newly tinted with a glint of red in it, too. She was only about a foot taller than I was, and the seventy years that she had already lived had left designs on her skin like the thread patterns in lace. She'd regally descend down the bus steps carefully carrying a cake tin with the fruitcake in it. She made it from a recipe that her own mother had handed down to her. It called for the cake to be heavily laced with brandy and to be wrapped in cheesecloth soaked in wine, even though no one in my grandmother's family believed in drinking spirits of any kind. Over the holidays she'd eat most of the cake herself, then get back on the bus in early January on the same day that I had to go back to school.

Later when I married, I found myself in places on Christmas where the turkey stuffing didn't have in it even so much as one crumb of cornbread, and fruitcakes hadn't even touched wine. That, of course, gave my grandmother a good excuse to say I was cohabitating with the Yankees.

On one Christmas Eve when I was living in Boston, my grandmother called me. "Bare bark. Horseradish. Mincemeat. And get home," she said, then hung up. I knew she was telling me that the trees in her yard had lost all their leaves, which she liked to say made them look as though they were the lead of pencils trying to write on the sky. I also knew that she had gotten her hands on some fine shrimp and was making horseradish sauce to dip them in, that she was baking a mincemeat pie to go along with her fruitcake, and also that she missed me.

After the birth of my second child, when I was living in Nebraska, my grandmother sent me the recipe for her fruitcake by registered mail. I think she'd given up on my moving back to the South, and she was becoming too feeble to properly make the fruitcake, which could easily take more than a day.

Now that I have lived in Florida for twenty years, I've thought about making a phone call to my grandmother this Christmas, if I could reach her. "Camellias. Water bowls. Bethlehem. Pool-side," I'd say. For I'd want her to know that I am here where the camellias are blooming deep Christmas red, or else snow white, or even as delicately pink as the inside of a cat's ear, and that we frequently float them in bowls of water on the coffee table. I want her to know that Christmas here in Florida must be much like the first one in

Bethlehem — with the sand and palm trees and with not much of a need for more than a sweater or swaddling clothes. And I think she'd get a kick out of knowing, too, that I am faithfully serving her fruit cake, poolside.

Dear Juan

During my childhood in Arkansas, all of our lives were lived to the rhythm of cotton growing. Plants were chopped free of weeds, and then small planes flew low over them to dust them with insecticides. By late summer, cotton fiber could be seen peeking out of the gray-brown bolls like jack rabbit tails. Then finally, on long sticky fall days, the cotton was gathered in big bags that trailed from the workers' shoulders. This is when the Mexicans came.

Whole truckloads of them would arrive for the picking season. They would stay for about two months, then leave as quickly as they had come. One day when I was ten, and it was a month after the Mexicans had left, I stopped into the post office on my way home from school. As soon as I opened the box to take out my family's mail, I saw the Post Master's eye looking back at me.

"I got something you might want," he said, and grinned. He slid a wrinkled sealed envelope through to me. "It's been here more than a month," he told me. "No return address. Just general delivery. I thought you might want it."

The Post Master giving me a letter might not have been legal, and my taking it could have landed us both in jail, I guess. But no harm was meant. And anyway, what was behind all this was the belief that I knew Spanish. For one year my family had moved up to Kansas where it was taught in the schools. And when I moved back, the rumor that I could speak Spanish spread all over town. I didn't have the heart or honesty to tell anybody that the most I could remember was how to sing *La Cucaracha*. So I took the letter home and hunted up my father's college Spanish dictionary.

I couldn't match one word in that letter to anything in that dictionary. And over the weeks, the mystery of the letter became the center of my life. It was a hot passionate note, I decided. There was news in it about a murder, and stolen money, and a loving woman who waited in Mexico for a handsome man who was picking cotton in Arkansas while things blew over. I slipped the letter into my father's dictionary and left it there.

Forty years later, when my father died, I inherited his library. Recently when I was placing his books on the shelves with my own books, I picked up that Spanish dictionary. And the letter fell out. It is dated November 3, 1954. It is written in pencil on notebook paper. But forty years has not faded much of what was meant to be said by someone in Mexico to someone in Arkansas who was picking cotton. I'm smarter now, so I took the letter to my son's high school for his Spanish teacher to read to me.

Dear Juan,
   I received your letter with the money in it. Then I received your letter yesterday asking for some of it back. Too late — I spent it. I was sick last week and went to the clinic. There I saw your old girlfriend. She called me a dog. I said you and she were dogs too. So now I tell no one how much money you send me. They ask to borrow, and I tell them that last time you sent me 30 pesos. Then they leave me alone. But no matter. I spent it all anyway.
   I wait for you. You say you will leave November 4th. So... Love, Gabrina

It has occurred to me that I might have kept Juan from knowing Gabrina spent all his money. And if I did, I'm sorry. But then, there had been no forwarding address. And Gabrina had mailed the letter only the day before she knew Juan would be leaving. So maybe Gabrina was only planning to say she had at least tried to warn him.

Juan and Gabrina are over sixty-five years old by now — if they are still alive. And their marriage must be over forty — if they are still together.

In a sense, their letter really was a love letter. And if they ever want to know, it is still here, safe, with me. I keep it in my father's dictionary with the pages closed tightly around it, just where it has been through all these years.

First Job

I remember my first job the same way I remember swallowing a cube of ice. It was painful, and there was nothing I could do about it, but just wait it out. It was not something, either, that I would want to readily admit I had done.

Actually, my very first job could have been to model scuba diving gear on an island in the Mississippi River. I was sixteen when two men in suits that could shine in the dark offered me $2.75 an hour to do that. When my mother found out that I would be strapping on the scuba gear over nothing but a bikini, she opened my eyes to the fact that breathing gear was not what this was all about. Oh — those were the days! The days which are even hard now to realize existed when the classified ads for employment were broken down into two parts: MALE HELP and FEMALE HELP.

When I got out of college, I set my sights high. I marched myself down to the Nashville Tennessean and said I wanted to be a reporter. It was 1966, and I was dressed in a navy blue dress with white gloves and wore blue leather shoes with silver buckles — lord help me, this is true — and I stood there dressed like that and said I knew women writing for newspapers mostly got to do the social news or the obituaries, but I intended to do other things. The man sitting there behind the desk in the personnel office might have been impressed with my chutzpah but instead he said that nobody in the whole place got a job without first passing an I.Q. test.

Now maybe it makes sense that anybody writing for a newspaper ought to pass an I.Q. test. But it sure wasn't the thing for me.

You see, early on in the fourth grade when I moved to Kansas and was given an I.Q. test to see just which class I should be put into, I found out that my intelligence was one that could never be measured. I'd like to say it was because it went off the charts. But that wasn't it. It was just that simply for every question, I could see a million answers. They all looked good to me. Later I took comfort in learning how Picasso never could do math because to him all the noses looked like upside down 7's. So on the day I was handed the newspaper's I.Q. test, I sat down at a table across from the personnel man, took off my gloves and filled in half the blanks willy-nilly. And that was that. I didn't even get offered the obituaries.

Instead I took a job at a local college where the dean's secretary locked me into a vault where all the files of past applications were kept. I was told to go through them one by one and make a list of how many people had applied from the North, how many from the South, how many from the East, and so on all the way across the world. At lunch time, the secretary came again to let me out, and then at 5 P.M., she came again.

So last night when the phone rang and I picked it up, and this fake cheerful but really depressed voice — you could tell — of some young person asked me if I would answer a few questions for one of those research telemarketing things, or whatever they call it, I said, "Is this your first job?"

"Well, yeah," the startled young thing said.

"And is it just driving you crazy?"

"Well, yeah," the startled young thing said again.

"So okay. Shoot." I said. "I'm going to give you the next fifteen minutes of my undivided time. And then after that, you have to promise — don't ever call me again."

Tilly

Tilly came to work at my house when my son was four. It was the year when I was overwhelmed by laundry and dusty woodwork and before computers, so that whatever I wrote had to be pecked out during children's naps or while they ate cookies in the knee-hole of my desk. Tilly was one of the few people who knew what I was up to.

At first she came to my house once every other week. And then once a week. She kept it up for over eight years. All that time, she never let me think that I was crazy or lazy for spending whole hours turning words into stories. In fact, she was the one who always said when she knew the writing business was going bad, "I've never known you to quit," — and this in spite of the fact she told me that she herself had quit school after the eighth grade, and, whenever she took a phone message for me, always added, "Hope I spelled enough of it right."

She showed me the ramshackle wooden building grown over with brush and big oaks where she had gone to school as a child. It was set behind a church. It was the only school black people had in our part of town in the 1920s.

Her grown children were ashamed, I think, that she was working in my house with all the appearances of being a maid. She wore white uniforms to my house, and I was ashamed of that, too. I preferred calling her A Mother's Helper, or a Disaster Aide. But Tilly never understood this.

At 10:00 A.M. everyday she had what she called a Gatorade Minute. She'd sit down with a glass of Gatorade over ice and say it was good not just for football players but was good for giving other people pep too. She loved to iron and would turn on the daytime soaps with the ironing board set up in front. Sometimes to make what she called "her stories" come out even with the ironing, she'd run over our underwear and fold them as if they were supposed to fit into an envelope.

She took great pride in whenever I dressed my children up. And when I put my son in one of his short pantsuits for his fifth birthday party, she stepped back from the ironing board and grinned. "Now doesn't he look fit to go sportin'?"

I loved that — fit to go sportin'. And whenever one of those late afternoon rains would come down so hard that I knew she had no business trying to walk to the bus stop to get home, she would say, "Yes sir, this is going to be a frog-strangler for sure." I would drive her home, all the while unable to get out of my mind the image of frogs lying in puddles gasping for air. It seemed so right that I was beginning to wonder which of us was the most fit to be the writer.

We moved one year. Not far — just from one house to a bigger one. After all, the kids were getting bigger, and it seemed time to do that. So it was up to me and Tilly to get one household moved five miles away to the next one. On the third day of our packing, I looked at Tilly across a nearly full box and said, "You know, I'm so hungry, I think I could eat cardboard."

"Don't get started on this, then," she said, and closed up the box.

We put it in the car with a whole load of others, left a space in the back for the dog, and headed to the new house. But on the way, I pulled into McDonald's and instead of going through the Drive-Thru, I parked and led Tilly inside. I had the distinct feeling that she was holding back. Then, when we got our trays and sat down, Tilly wouldn't eat. Her discomfort was so evident, it was almost as if I could taste it. But she didn't say anything. She only let it be known that she wanted to save part of her sandwich for the dog, who was so patiently waiting in the car outside.

I started thinking of the day years before when, as soon as Tilly had come to work at my house, she had asked me rather breathlessly to do her a favor. "Will you drive me downtown?" she had asked, then pointed the way in the car until we pulled up into the parking lot of the funeral home on the north side of town. "Will you come in with me?" she asked. It was then that I had put two and two together, for she was there for the viewing of one of her other employers who had died the day before. And like me, the employer was white. And this was the white people's funeral home. And Tilly was afraid to go into it without someone like me along. I guess Death is still the most segregated of passages. So that's how I ended up sitting in a room with a group of grieving people I'd never met before.

Now as Tilly and I sat in McDonald's across from each other, I saw that it was just this — sitting here with me in public felt so very wrong to her. Old habits are hard on digestion. So we took our sandwiches out to the car and ate small bites off of them and threw other small bites into the back for the dog.

But this is what seems strange: over all the years that Tilly worked in my house, whenever she arrived while I was driving the kids to school, I'd come in the back door and yell out, "Tilly?" And from one of the back bedrooms where she'd be changing the sheets, she'd call back, "Yooo-hoooo," in exactly the same way my grandmother used to. In fact, if I listened to that sound only, I would think it was my grandmother back there in the bedrooms calling out to me. So I have a retrieval system now. Tilly is in the last years of her life, and I call her every month or so. As I listen, I hear in her voice echoes of past generations in my own family. Different times. Different people. Different colors. Different beliefs. But so much of it the same.

We talk a long while now, Tilly and I, on the phone, rehashing memories as we pull up the past we shared together. In most ways, she has become a mother to me, now that I am her age when she first came to my house, and she is the age of my grandmother the last time I saw her. And Tilly never fails to ask, "Now tell me, how's that dog? And your next book — when's it coming out? And now I want to know exactly, just where's that son of yours sportin' this week?".

Costumes

When my children were little, one of the greatest stresses I suffered was getting them dressed up and out the door as whoever they'd decided to be on October 31. Somewhere in the middle of September, I began daily praying that my children were harboring secret desires to be a cowboy or a witch or a ghost for Halloween, something that I could whip up out of the linen closet or toy bin in a flat half hour, and that would be that. But nope, nothing simple ever tripped through my children's imaginations, no matter how much I withheld their sugar intake or TV.

One year, my son decided to be a table. We covered him with a checkered cloth and glued a wine bottle to his head. He wasn't just any table, he was a corner table in an Italian restaurant. And he played an accordion under the cloth and sang Amoré.

For a fair number of years, we went on like this, with them thinking up being broken down cars or some sort of plumbing equipment or the CEO of GM, which no one could guess until they handed out calling cards and tried to sell stock certificates. The night before Halloween there'd they'd be, sleeping like little angels, and I'd be up half the night doing the final paper-machéing or pushing the old sewing machine into hyperthrust until it smoked.

Other mothers on my same street talked about it, too —how we would send the kids out to trick or treat, usually with some dad as escort who was happy to throw a king-sized sheet over his head and be done with it, while we mothers would flop back on the couch with more exhaustion than what even Christmas could do to us.

My revenge was my haunted house. It wasn't a special haunted house, it was just my house. Whenever the little neighborhood darlings would ring my door bell and sweetly call out, "Trick or Treat," I lowered a galvanized watering trough down from the roof and let them dig into it for roasted peanuts and boxes of raisins and packages of celery sticks and caramelized broccoli. I was known as a real bummer.

There is no costume for this. You can be a real bummer in just about anything in your closet.

I have to admit, though, over the years Halloween became one of my favorite holidays. As my children got older they took responsibility for expressing their own imaginations, and I had time then to express more of my own.

This year I've decided to be a bench in an old timey bus station, like the kind I grew up with in the 50s. Don't ask me why. And don't try to test my slats. I could use a little help with the paper-maché and brown paint, though. And then, I'm just going to plant myself somewhere and watch everybody else pass by.

Cupcakes and the Law

When I moved here in 1979, I signed up to be my daughter's homeroom mother. For the next ten years, I stayed a homeroom mother. And all those years of homeroom motherdom got me into trouble with the law.

The first time was when my son started the first grade. Of course by then I'd honed my homeroom skills on his sister. So I knew you don't make those cupcakes for the class party. No, instead you go to Publix and buy them. That year on the day of the Halloween party, apparently a lot of other homeroom mothers had wised up, too. I guess nobody wanted to stay up the night before baking stuff that might turn out lopsided or not nearly so cute as what the Publix bakery could do. My plan was to deliver the cupcakes to the school at the same time I dropped my son off, then go home and write a novel. So at 7 A.M. on the morning of Halloween, my son and I were standing in line at the Publix bakery waiting to pick up our pumpkin-decorated cupcakes, when he asked, "Is this going to make us ate?" I knew he meant to say late, but he had no front teeth, so there was nothing for his tongue to make an L against. "No way," I said, "We'll never be late."

I wish I hadn't made that promise.

By the time we got our cupcakes and were headed to the station wagon where the dog was hanging her head out the back window, it was ten minutes from the sound of the first bell. I jockeyed out onto Newberry Road and aimed all 300 horsepower toward my son's school. Now, I have a bad habit, and that's that I never remember to look into the rear-view mirror. I guess I could have my driver's license revoked for this.

But we all know it's hard being perfect, and this is pretty much my only flaw. I think it's just that I never much care about where I've been. I look only straight ahead, which is why ambulances and fire trucks follow me for miles while using odd rhythms with their sirens. Then when I finally get the idea and pull off the road, they pass me with a look that tells me I am mud.

So on the day I was delivering the Halloween cupcakes, it was no surprise that a police car began following us. It kept it up for quite some time until it sped up and put on its siren and lights, which finally made the dog howl. I guess by then the policeman driving it was thinking we were hauling hot goods.

While the police officer walked toward our car, I rolled down my window. My son leaned up behind my headrest and breathed onto my neck and asked, "Are we going to prison?"

"Not today," I said.

The police officer took off his dark glasses and leaned in toward us. The dog would have taken the top part of his head off if I hadn't put a cupcake in her mouth. "Where you going so fast?" he asked.

"School," I said, and then my son screamed out, "And we're nearly ate."

"Yes, nearly late," I added, then handed the police officer a cupcake while he wrote out my speeding ticket.

That afternoon when the dog and I picked my son up, I asked him how the party had gone.

"Oh, all right," he said. But nothing was as good as that morning at Show and Tell when he told everybody how I nearly got us sent to prison.

First Day

Oh, that first day of school. There was so much to get ready for. And so much to argue about. I also knew that once my kids and I started setting the alarm and getting out of our lazy summer habits, we'd be forever afterward too worn out to shop for new clothes, or lunch box food, or notebook paper. We wouldn't have the strength, either, to argue about how to keep lunch box sandwiches cool so that food poisoning wouldn't make them miss the whole first week of school anyway. So before D- Day, my kids and I hit the mall, and the grocery store, and the army/navy supply.

That first day outfit is no fly-by-night decision. In fact, your self worth for the rest of your life is riding on how you come off with that first day appearance. Dress like a nerd, and you will be a nerd for the rest of your life — even if one day in the middle of the year you pull off all your clothes and turn up in homeroom naked. Yep, dressing wrong on the first day is a mistake that no power in the universe can erase. Sales clerks know this too, and that's why they are so obliging. Half of them didn't make it through the first day themselves, and so that's why they so silently pick up mounds of clothes off the floor in dressing rooms and hang them back up with nary a peep.

The problem is, there is no prescribed formula for what is cool on that first day. One year it can be knickers or shorts, a mini skirt or overalls — at least if you're a girl. For boys it can be jeans that are belted six inches above the knees, or khakis with a crease, or shorts big enough for two. Who knows? There are rumors, of course. And my kids used to study these like they never did their books.

My favorite memory is the year my son started kindergarten. Thank goodness coolness isn't much of a factor when you are five. The issues then are more like can you make it through the day without wetting your pants, and will you have at least one friend who will hold your hand when you line up for the lunchroom, and can you remember where to go to get your ride home?

The week before my son started kindergarten, we were in a department store where he got so excited he twirled around a rack of clothes until all the pant legs were airborne. I was busy with his older sister who was fretting over should she choose Guess shorts or Guess jeans, and while I said I guessed either one would do, my son took seven outfits — one for each day of the week — and bolted into a dressing room. I was pretty proud that he even knew there were seven days in a week. But when I looked in on him, I found him standing in a pair of size 10 orange striped pants and a purple turtleneck that went up over his chin. The other six outfits were strewn on the floor. And from each one he had pulled off every tag. Those outfits were ours, for better or for worse, because I just didn't have the heart to tell the sales clerks what he had done. I also believed he could grow into his mistakes.

But all the years my kids were in school, what kept me up nights was how to keep their lunches from poisoning them. Because how do you keep sandwiches cool when it is no longer cool to take a lunch box? In a lunch box you can put cold paks. And up until the sixth grade, I outfitted my kids with stuff from the army/navy store. They had five course dinners fit for a fox hole, but by sixth grade, paper sacks were all that would do. Hang a lunch box on your arm, and you'd never go to the prom.

I used frozen drinks and memorized the lethal bacteria count for tuna fish. But it didn't matter. Because a few years after my first child graduated from high school, she confessed to me that every day for six years she had been throwing away her packed lunch and buying crackers out of a vending machine.

Thank goodness they don't tell you these things too soon.

End-of-the-Year Programs

There's nothing like an end-of-the-year school program to make you wish you'd never been fertile. Or to make you wish you'd had about a hundred and two children and could just keep on going. In fact, there's no middle ground when it comes to late May and your kid is standing up in the back line of a first-grade play singing his heart out through a toothpick space between his two new front teeth. Or else he is the only one standing on the front row with his lips sewn together as tight as the spandex waistband on his underpants.

I remember how a good friend of mine went into a deep depression after she went to her daughter's kindergarten end-of-the-year program, and her child was the only one who refused to sing. "What is wrong with her?" she later confided in me with a little hysterical tone in her voice.

I don't know why she asked me. My daughter was the only one who, at the first of the year, had forgotten her lines in the Halloween play and had to be prompted by two teachers and her own mother. Yes, I was the one who suddenly stood up in the middle of the third row and gave hand signals and mouthed the words that my daughter and I had practiced for five nights and three afternoons. What else was I supposed to think but that a mysterious virus had passed through the school and stolen my daughter's brain when all she had to say was, "Boo said the ghost. The pumpkin, too. Boo."

But then, there is something really quite wonderful when your child is the star of the show and remembers all of his lines, or else is given none to learn in the first place. It was a terrific year when my son played the title role in the kindergarten play as a piece of wheat. I joyfully watched him get watered and fed and warmed by the sun. Then I tearfully sat through the scene of his getting mowed down, harvested and turned into bread.

The other day I went to the end-of-the-year first grade play where my daughter is now a teacher. I watched a seven-year old, who was playing the title role as a crab, molt and evade a sea snake who was made up of three boys under a cotton snake skin — the head of which gave a whole new meaning to a snake's tongue. The molting crab taught the entire audience about his under-the-sea lifestyle, but my heart really went out to the sea anemone who couldn't remember what to say when the crab asked him did he like living in the ocean near the coral reef. After a few long seconds, he finally let it out, "Yes I do. I really do." It was said as fine as a congressman at a congressional investigation, too.

I guess I've never been to any show where the players and the audience are so clearly connected. You can look around the room and see all sorts of ages of people — mothers, grandmothers, fathers taking an hour off from work — all of them perched on the ends of their seats with their breaths held. A lot of them keep their faces covered up by the black shapes of cameras, too.

I know that's the way I was able to sit through my son's first band concert when he was in middle school. The black eye of the camera was the only dry one in the house when those trumpet players and a whole row of trombones stood up and played their first notes with their cheeks popped out like cantaloupes. I don't think I've ever witnessed a display of such determined human effort.

But then, it was nice too, to still be hidden behind the camera when the rest of the brass section sat down and my son was the only one still standing up playing a whole long measure that everybody else had finished a while before. It was a nice measure though. It had at least five different notes in it. And well, he did it with such gusto.

Suits

When my son turned twelve, he took a hankering for a suit. So we went to shop for one.

Back then, he came up to my shoulder. I could still beat him at arm wrestling, and I had to drive him to wherever he wanted to go. But in the department store, as we headed to the Young Men's Section, whenever we came to a counter, he would duck off onto the opposite side from me, even though I was his sole support for his next meal and his ride home.

I took the hint, and after I set him up with a clerk who opened up a dressing room for him, I hung out by the ties as though I were just some strange lady who had followed him there. The clerk took suit after suit into the dressing room, and then finally my son appeared in a nice navy blue pinstripe. When he spotted me, he came walking my way with his pant legs flapping over his white crew socks spattered with soccer field mud. "Oh, that's nice," I said.

"I don't like it," he announced.

"But it really looks nice," I reassured him.

"No," he told me. "It isn't what I wanted."

I held up one of the ties off the table. "It only needs a little something like this," I suggested. But as he looked past me, his eyes landed on something high up behind me. "That's it," he said. "That's the one I want."

I turned around to look at the suit that apparently had been in his mind the whole time. It was hanging near the ceiling on a hook by itself. It was light gray with fat black stripes up and down it, and the material had a sheen to it like the sides of a fish. It was what I had seen in the movies in my childhood being worn by bookies and con men and gangsters who got a thrill out of pushing somebody into wet concrete.

"I don't think that's your size," I said.

But before my words even reached him, he was having the saleslady wiggle the suit off its hook with a long-handled spear as though she were gaffing a shark. Then he trotted off into the dressing room with it.

Twenty minutes later we were walking out of the department store with that suit inside of a see-through plastic bag that, for a while, I carried, since I was taller, then passed off to him when we got to the shoe section where I saw someone I knew.

At home, my son hung the suit in his closet for a week. That next Friday night when he was dressing in it, I was wondering how composed could I sit during his class graduation while he walked across the stage with all the other parents wondering, "Did she buy him that suit?" Or "Wonder why she let him buy that suit?"

Suddenly there was a cry in my son's room, and he appeared in the doorway wearing his new suit and holding up his hand. "There's a hole in it," he said. "Look, there's a hole in it!"

His words seemed a little rehearsed to me. I looked at his sleeve, where indeed, in the place where the label on the suit had once been was now a gaping hole. Instantly I knew that he had tried to remove the label with a pair of scissors and had not realized what a delicate operation that required. He was embarrassed to tell me the truth, so was just going to pass it off as a defect — a defect which we had unknowingly bought and carried out of the store.

"Oh, I'm so sorry," I lied. "Should we take it back?"

"Naw," he said. "If we were dumb enough to buy it this way, I guess we ought to keep it. I can still wear the pants."

I picked up the car keys, and we got in the car. The dog sat down in the driveway and watched us drive off without her. I glanced over at the pants that seemed to light up the whole front seat. But I was really fortunate, I knew, that it had come down to this — appearing in public with a gangster from only the waist down.

Deer Secrets

What gets to me about turning fifty is that everything on my body is moving south. Eventually it will be Gravity 10 and Body Parts 0. But meanwhile, I have been walking the dog for a mile every morning, then coming back and swimming for fifteen minutes.

The dog makes me go; she needs her walk. And then she sits on the side of the pool and watches me swim as she pants. She hates water as much as I do; we are both land animals. But she is still young and doesn't really give a flip about how she looks in her clothes, so she patiently watches over me while I kick and paddle and try to tighten and relift myself.

Last spring I ordered a bathing suit from the Victoria's Secret Catalog. It was partly the sneer on the model's face on page 50 that dared me to whip out my Visa and order by phone what she barely had on. The fact that the page number and my age matched was no small potatoes, either. And when it came, I hid it in the cushions of the couch in the family room.

When the weather got warm, I pulled it out and pulled it on. It was small and black with a sheen to it like racing silks. It covered the subject, but that was about all. In fact, my whole changing geography was on display.

For a while, I smartly wore a big shirt over it while I walked my dog. But then when the days got so hot, and I became so lazy (which I prefer to call mellowed out) I began walking my dog in it and even leaving her leash at home so I could quickly come back and jump straight into the pool.

It's a good thing I live on a retired watermelon farm. Tucked back into jungly woods, my house sits in a mess of greens. Old single lane roadbeds wind through the hammock like a handful of loose ribbon, and even though these wild acres leak into the fancy housing developments that are now rising around me like good yeast rolls, I can still go whole days without being seen.

Yesterday, though, my dog and I came upon a stranger. We were halfway down one of our sandy roads when a deer came out of the woods and stood in front of us. It was a doe, and I looked at her, and she looked at me, then moved her eyes quickly to my dog. My dog looked at the deer and then sat down and looked up at me and whined. We all knew it was in my dog's nature to run after the deer, to bring her down, to kill and eat her. Or at the least scare the bejesus out of her, so she'd end up miles from here. And I knew that if I moved suddenly, the deer might frantically bound off over the fence rows and head toward the highway, for she was probably already at the farthest end of the last few acres of her home. It wasn't really in her nature to be living here on the edge of a new housing development with paved driveways and swimming pools.

As though in a rehearsed dance, we each, all three of us, moved one foot at a time. In movements so slow it seemed we were traveling above earth, we parted, until the deer was safely camouflaged in the trees, my dog was walking beside me just past where the leaves had closed over the deer, and I was once again on the middle of the sandy road heading nowhere but to walk against the natural course of my own aging.

Since then, at least a half dozen times, we've met again: me and my dog, and the deer. Each time we have looked at each other, then slowly passed. For none of us dares to blab our secrets — not a word about my dog's faint heart, or the deer's willing accommodation to suburbia, or my Victoria's Secret swimsuit that looks so good on page 50.

A Cowgirl at the Last Minute

My stockbroker has always told me never to buy anything that eats while I'm asleep. But in the final weeks of the summer before my daughter was leaving for college, I decided to. I bought a horse.

I was rounding the last few bases before sliding into fifty, and it seemed to me I needed to remember who I was when I started out. I don't think this is so uncommon — to reach back into childhood and dust off an old passion and squeeze it back into life. And so I don't think this is so odd — becoming a cowgirl, even if it is at the last minute.

I hadn't even sat on a horse in more than ten years, but I figured that if I could lift my leg high enough to get on one, I would definitely be doing fine. So on a day when no one at home or anywhere else seemed to need me, I went to a local horse show to see if I might come upon one that might do. For a long while, I sat in the arena watching the horses and their riders go round and round. Sometimes they moved together, and sometimes they bounced against each other — somewhat resembling microwave corn popping against the sides of its bag — and then they'd usually settle down. As I watched them, I began to know what it is about horses that makes me so passionate about them. It's not only their obvious beauty and grace and stoicism. Whenever I've read anything written about them, such as the recent beautiful passages by Cormac McCarthy in which he describes man's attraction to them because of their ardentheartedness, what he calls, "the heat of the blood that ran them," I know that what I feel for them is quite a bit less refined, but yet no less spiritual. For as I sat in the arena that day and watched all of those horses going round and round, sweating, working something fierce to do whatever the people on their backs were asking them to do, I suddenly realized that not one of those horses knew where he was going. Instead, each one had placed all of his belief in the hope that whoever was on his back did know. And also I knew that the human sitting up there didn't — not really. The people riding were going round and round, enjoying it, but doing so because someone had made them believe it was something they should do. And so there it was — a realization about my own life and the serenity I could gain in accepting it for just what it was — a ride of uncertain destination.

I looked over at the entrance gate just as horse number 17 was walking into the arena. He was going pretty slow. In fact, he was going so slow that his front leg had barely swung out of the way before his back leg came up to claim the dirt where it had been. But when the commands came out over the microphone, he got all of himself going pretty good. Then right after he lined up in front of the judge, he fell asleep.

"This might be a horse I can ride," I thought. When he was announced as having won second place over a handful of others, and that he was up for sale, I got up to follow him out. I stood for a while on the other side of the show grounds so I could just look over at him. He was standing in a huddle with some others near a corral. He was white. And he had a teenager on his back. Right away, I felt a connection.

He was moving his tail in a slow fly-swatter beat that reminded me of the hand of my grandmother on her fan in church. And since his eyes were already once again halfway closed, he didn't even see me coming.

I asked the people who owned him all the right questions. After all, I'm no dummy. I knew how low my ability was. Yes, even a child could ride him, they told me. And yes, he could go down the road, come upon a jogger or someone on a bicycle and not go bonkers and sling me off. He was twelve years old, and by horse years that put him and me at about the same age. He was a quarter horse, which meant he could run faster than almost anything for a quarter of a mile, and on any given day could catch a cow, if he really wanted to. He'd also been owned by a child since he was four. I knew what that felt like.   .

His name was Skip, which wasn't exactly Silver. But it started with an S. And at my age, Silver could be embarrassing. He would also cost me in initial investment about the same as purchasing a 20-year-old classic Ford Mustang, which was a good measure of an acceptable mid-life crisis, and in upkeep, probably about the same.

I made an appointment to go out to where he lived and to look him over again and try him out. I walked off and looked back once more. He was still asleep.

He didn't know it yet, but I wanted more out of him than just a memory of my childhood and a sense of serenity. I wanted him to make me take the time to go through the land, to make me take the time to hear and smell and feel the world I was living in. I wanted him to exercise more than just my arms and legs and back. I wanted him to exercise my right to remember who I was after so many years of being a wife and a mother —

which by necessity and the joy of doing those jobs well — required that my senses be attuned to those I cared for. I wanted him to make me take a slow ride.

On that part, he was obviously keen.

Getting On

Yesterday I had Skip delivered to me. I braided his mane and tail any way I wanted to, and he didn't care — something my daughter rarely allowed. It is early morning and I am like a young mother who wakes in the middle of the night when her newborn only turns over. I am so attuned to the fact that Skip now knows he is mine and that he depends on me and my kindness; I have hurried to be with him at the stable where I am boarding him.

I take him out of his pasture and lead him near the tack room where I am keeping my brand new thirty-eight pound western saddle with silver plate and floral carving. To get it onto his back I have to raise it over my head in a clean-and-jerk maneuver. And once I get it up there, I still have to lift my leg high enough to get on. I have to remember to save something for that.

With a short lead rope, I tie Skip to a ring outside of the tack room. But just as I snap the rope to the wall, some primeval instinct runs through his mind. He thinks he is caught, caught for good in this strange new barn where, heaven knows, a lion or tiger could jump down onto his back from the rafters overhead. He pulls against the lead rope, goes down on his haunches, breaks the copper snap into two pieces, and apparently my ring finger with it.

For a minute, we just lie here on the floor. What silly thing have we done to ourselves?

I look around, embarrassed. Luckily no one else is here. We get up, both of us shaking. My ring finger is now the size of a Cuban cigar.

I lead Skip around to see if he walks okay. He seems to. So I saddle him by tying him in a stall and carrying the saddle farther than I'd wanted to. We're just not going to mention any of this to anyone. Fingers. Falls. Who? Not us.

I can see about the finger later.

Outside in the riding ring, I get on by pulling myself up, using my good four fingers in a handful of Skip's mane. The sun is lemon yellow now and warm, and I can't help but want to leave the safety of the riding ring and try the road.

We move down it slowly. Not since my childhood have I allowed myself the leisure of leaving tasks undone. Letters unanswered. Dishes in the sink. But here I am with no destination in mind, and with Skip as symbol. Skip the dishes. Skip the bills. Skip the laundry and all those tasks that can swell to steal hours until I can feel I have accomplished nothing at all.

The sneeze weeds are blooming like tiny white stars in the ditches beside us. Their musty smell flirts with the smell of our new leather. The crows holler at us from overhead, calling us names. But I know they are only jealous. For Skip and I are learning valuable things. Clearly, he is not as dead as I had thought when I bought him. And he also knows I don't give a fig about going as fast as that teen-ager who owned him before me.

To the slow beat of his hooves, a rhyme trickles through my mind — a poem I learned in my childhood that over and over I recited to my own children at bedtime when they were very small. (Fuzzy, bunny-like sleepers, mouths sucking like the waves of a tide.)

Ride a cock horse to Banbury Cross.

To see a fine lady upon a white horse.

Rings on her fingers and bells on her toes.

And she shall have music wherever she goes.

My wedding ring now is like a tiny ditch in my swollen finger. And there are no bells on my toes. No map in sight to Banbury Cross, either. But with a choir of crows, and doubts about sometimes qualifying as a lady, still, I am fine.

For this morning, anyway. Fine.

Stalled

I've put my horse, Skip, on a diet. We've taken up being in horse shows, and I've figured out a whole lot about how to win.

The first weekend that we went to one, on Saturday, the judge was named Buck, and he gave us fourth place. On Sunday, the judge was named Goose. And I put on diamond earrings to set off my white Resitol cowboy hat. I wore green chaps and painted my finger-nails bright Watermelon Pink so they'd look nice holding the reins. Goose gave us first place. It was clear, he liked his women trashy.

But now I am stumped. At all the horse shows lately Skip and I have been coming in last. I've narrowed the problem down to one single and stinging fact. It's that neither he nor I can any longer hold our stomachs in.

Last week, I cut back on his feed and put him in a stall for the whole day to keep him off grass. I put myself on tomato juice and Ritz crackers five times a day.

But after a week of that, neither Skip nor I look much better, and both of us are mean. We don't even like each other anymore.

When I go out to see him, he bolts out of his stall the minute I open it. And while I chase after him, I remind him that I am hungry enough to eat a horse. He looks up where he is munching grass, just out of my reach. He used to neigh this sweet little sound of endearment at me, like he was strumming a bass guitar string low in his throat, but now I hear him mumbling under his breath that I am an old nag who's gonna starve him to death. When he walks away, I get a bucket with just enough feed in it to make a sound when I drip it out of my fingers, so he thinks I have a lot.

Of course when he walks over to investigate, I nab him. And then I put on the saddle and cinch it up, making a notch beside the hole that is our goal for the end of the month.

But when we get out into the woods and start riding across open fields, everything we see seems to remind us of food. The way the birds are flitting from tree to tree chattering about where the best worms are. The way the egrets sit behind cattle waiting with the patience of Job. Even the way the trees lean toward the light. Everything in the whole world seems to be eating except us.

I don't know that it's even possible for Skip and me at our ages to tighten ourselves up. I mean between us, we add up to over sixty-five years. By now we ought to have lost that razor edge of wanting to win and of hearing our names called out on some microphone in some arena somewhere.

When we get back to the barn, I go into the tack room and take out a box of sugar lumps that I have hidden under a floorboard. I lead him out into the middle of the field where the egrets are and the leaning trees and the busy birds, and we each suck one — and only one — sugar lump like there is no tomorrow so that the desire for just one more is like a small fire inside us. Because the truth is, I figure that when we have given up the razor edge of wanting something, we will be old.

95

Mares

It seems the closer I got to fifty, the wilder I became. For a while even Skip and I were bored with each other. And so on the spur of the moment, I flew out to Oklahoma and bought myself an Appaloosa horse at the National Championship. I declared that I would take her back there the following year and ride her myself. I would sell her then. That was my plan.

I bought a mare because I figured that her mareness was an insurance policy of sorts. After all, she cost me nearly the whole advance I'd gotten on my second novel, so if she went lame, I was counting on the fact that she could at least still have babies, babies that I could sell.

Her name was Wiggles, since that's what she mostly did. Standing still was not her strong point.

All year I worked hard at learning to ride her, and she worked hard at trying to let me. When it came time to go to the National Championship, I spent as much time designing the outfit I would wear as I had spent on my own wedding dress. I was going to wear fancy fringed chaps and a brocaded jacket with jewels at my neck and matching ones for my ears. I bought myself a saddle with as much silver on it as if I had melted my grandmother's tea service down. Then the week before we were to leave, I gave Wiggles a hot oil treatment, which meant that I heated up six bottles of VO5 in a coffeepot and poured it over her.

It was a hot morning in July when I put Wiggles on a trailer headed to Oklahoma. "Don't let her lie down," I told the cowboy who was the driver. The point was, I wanted her tired when she got there.

I, myself, flew on an airplane to meet her. But when she arrived, she wasn't the least bit tuckered out. In fact, she was wiggling in her stall as if she'd flown out there First Class with her feet propped up.

On the day that I was to ride in my first event, I polished the saddle and Wiggles up so they were both about as shiny as a new dime. The whole time I had to keep reminding myself not to squat while I had on spurs. Then, since there were so many of us competing, cowboys lined up at the entrance to the arena like traffic cops motioning us to trot in one at a time. Country music played in the background — some song by Mary Chapin Carpenter about how you could wake up feeling lucky.

It was a great big arena, and it was air conditioned. When Wiggles hit the cool air, she jumped up and came down trotting in a whole new place.

Someone called out commands on a microphone, but it was all I could do to just keep Wiggles halfway aimed at where I wanted to go. We sideswiped one judge and came flat-out toward another, until he ran like a crab so as to let us miss him. When we were back on the rail, Wiggles stuck her nose in the backend of the horse in front and lifted her own rearend to kick at the one behind. Finally after we lined up in front of the judges, she set about wiggling so fiercely, I had to scratch her over her withers to keep her stranding in one spot

— except that that had its own side effect. For it was then that she lifted her head and rolled her upper lip up over her nose.

Outside the arena in the warm-up pen, I got off. I noticed that everyone was giving us a wide berth. In fact, a lot of people were watching us, and all the riders were making their horses walk in big circles way away from us. Especially the ones on stallions. And that's when it dawned on me what the real trouble was.

I walked over to the cowboy who had driven Wiggles there and handed him the reins. "Take her home," I said. "I'm going home, too." I stood and watched him lead Wiggles off, for I knew the truth. With a menopausal woman on a mare in heat, it was only a matter of time before everybody asked us to leave.

There You Have It

All down the hall in my house is a gallery of family pictures. Right there near the end is my daughter in her first prom dress, and my son with his first date. Choosing objects of desire is a funny business, I think. It starts out simple, like wanting a certain dollhouse, or wishing for a new truck. Then it gets lost in a chowder of hormones and diluted by the safety of choosing what everyone else wants. I remember getting my first crush after I went to a Saturday morning movie when I was five. That was in 1949 when ten cents could get you in for a whole double feature, and for hours you could watch cowboys ride over wide open plains after cows, or run around as part of a posse, chasing someone. My first crush was on Roy Rogers, and just about as equally on Trigger.

Apparently there's a good bit written down by Freud and people like that about this — about females and horses and that the connection between them is based on something sexual. But in my opinion all that is a bunch of hooey. Because I know something about growing up female. And what I know is that what girls most want to learn from horses has to do with survival.

Any horse manual you pick up will tell you that if you're walking forward leading one, and the dern thing balks, make him step in a different direction — even reach out and push his shoulder if you have to, just get him off balance — then lead him to where you really want to go. The point is: don't ever let him learn his own strength. Managing a thousand pound animal takes finesse. If he refuses to do something you have asked him to do, tuck one of his ears under the top strap of his bridle or halter, and by the time he gets it loose, he'll have forgotten what he didn't want to do in the first place. Remember — body posture is everything. Act like you know what you're doing and where you are going and he'll be inclined to follow you.

Now I can truthfully say that all of these techniques I have used on a horse at one time or another, and also at one time or another on some person — and most often a man. And if that means I have a sexual relationship with my horse, well, there you have it.

COWS

Apparently I'm not the only one bitten with the idea of living something of a cowgirl — or cowboy's — life. I have some good friends who, soon after their son went off to Duke, got cows. They can't say why, and they can't say why, either, they have named them after opera singers.

Maybe it's the size of the cows' chests, or the way they can stand in the back of the pasture and bellow as though their long lost love has gone off to McDonald's. But according to my friends, there is something in the general nature of the animal that wants to sing.

The first one they got was a black bull they named Carlo Bergonzi. Pretty soon they had a herd of eight cows who each night would meet my friends at the front gate as they drove home from work. Cows don't have much expression in general, but after a couple of months my friends said their cows developed definite moods that they felt compelled to read. In the evening, as soon as my friends pulled into their driveway, their cows would hang their heads over the fence and walk ever so slowly to escort the car into the garage. Along the way, my friends could look over each cow and talk about whether or not he or she was putting on weight, seemed to be happy, depressed, or looked antsy.

Apparently it's important to have a contented cow. If a cow is supposed to become meat or to give milk, it's best that the cow stay oblivious to all this and go on thinking he's out in green pastures forever and for no reason. These cows that my friends have are of the meat variety, bred to become T-bones, stew, and to appear in spaghetti. But when my friends' cows took on the names of Bergonzi and Pavarotti and Marilyn and Beverly, my friends became vegetarians. Now they are quick to give you their twenty-five recipes for beans.

Over the months, the cow herd has expanded and so has their relationship with my friends. Each night now the cows not only meet my friends and escort them to the garage, they also walk the fence line outside of the house, following my friends as they go from room to room. The herd begins at the kitchen, then moves on to the windows of the family room, then finally to the bedroom, until the last light is turned out.

The only problem my friends now have is that their cow herd is getting so big they recently had to give their backyard over to pasture. One night my friends were awakened by a baritone, or at least that's what they said. It was an impassioned singing followed by a loud crash like cymbals being used somewhere out in the pasture. When they turned on the back porch lights, they saw Bergonzi running at a charcoal grill. They had forgotten they had abandoned it in a corner of the patio that they had recently turned into pasture.

Bergonzi was running up under it, putting it over his horns and flipping it high into the air where it would do a somersault, then crash down. No doubt he was doing it for all the cows in the world.

But I didn't ask my friends what he was singing. I didn't need to. I'm pretty sure it was some kind of ode to joy. I'm also pretty sure that next week, when my friends drive up to see their son at Duke, they're going to ask me to baby-sit their cows.

Vacation

My best friend has gone on vacation and left me her dog. I don't much like her dog. It is little and yippy and reminds me of how I could feel when my kids were too young to park in front of Sesame Street for an hour every afternoon. I like big dumb dogs, the kind that won't fit in your lap. The ones that if you shut them up in a room with a bag of dog food can't figure out how to open it. Or, when you fuss at them for getting on the couch, they stay off of it even when you are gone. Not because they have a conscience, but because it takes them a couple of hours to figure out that you are gone.

I also don't like my friend's dog because he reminds me of my high school math teacher. He sits down there on the floor looking at me while I fix his dinner and everything on his face is saying, "You can do better than this." His name is Charley, the same name my math teacher had, and his teeth don't meet in the center either.

The day my friend flew off to a dude ranch in Montana, she drove Charley over to my house and left me with a whole long list of how to care for him. She was so afraid he would grieve over her leaving that she made him a tape. I was told to play it when he seemed agitated, and he would think she was there with him and everything would be all right.

Well, to me, Charley looks agitated all the time. So right off, I started playing the tape. Now, I know my friend likes me and has no reason whatsoever to try to qualify me for a loony bin. And I also believe that she loves her dog, I mean really, really loves him. So there'd be no reason for her to push me to the point of wanting to drive him over to some lake and pitch him in to an alligator. But I am starting to have these sorts of thoughts, and that's what scares me.

You see, I have played the tape now a total of twenty-three times, thinking each time will do the trick and Charley will calm down. But instead he keeps running around the house rooting under the couch and in all the closets and outside behind every tree and bush, looking for my friend. Give him two seconds of her voice on that tape, and he is like Richard Simmons leading aerobics.

Yesterday, I just couldn't take it anymore. I burned the tape right in front of Charley. I hid all the pictures of my friend, and I wouldn't even say a word that sounded like her name. Then I shut him up in the laundry room and went to the kitchen to call her.

"I'm having trouble with Charley." I said.

"Why?" she asked me.

"Well, he misses you," I said. "And he also reminds me too much of my high school math teacher. I'm starting to have bad thoughts about him."

"Oh, for heavens sakes," she said, "put him on the phone."

When I went to get him, I found him in the clothes hamper sniffing through the socks. I carried him to the phone and put the receiver over his ear. In a few minutes, he wiggled loose and calmly sat down at my feet and looked up at me.

I put the phone to my own ear. I was so afraid my friend was going to tell me to just suck it up and stick it out that I shut my eyes so I couldn't even see Charley.

But instead she said, "Okay. Put him on the flight out of there at 5:00 P.M. But I swear to goodness, sometimes the thing you most need a vacation from just up and follows you."

Me and My Bugs

I just got back from California. And if you want to know the truth, there is one thing about California that bothers me deep down in my bones. There are no bugs there.

I ate almost every one of my meals outside and didn't have to brush away flies. I sat out way past dusk without having to slap at any part of my body because a mosquito had landed on it. Maybe this is why California has sometimes been called paradise. I know my childhood friend Emmy Lou Taylor back in Arkansas told me that a lack of bugs was a necessary ingredient for paradise.

The day she explained bugs to me, we were standing on our heads, seeing who could do it the longest. I had my head mashed into a nice wad of Bermuda grass, and my feet were stuck up like poles, until some mosquito started buzzing around, trying to bite my toes. "Darn," I exclaimed when I lost my balance. "Why do we have to have stupid bugs in the first place!"

Emily Lou didn't even have to think. "To remind us," she said. She was still upside down with blood rushing to her face.

"Remind us of what?" I asked.

"Our fall," she said. I thought she was trying to rub in my loss of our headstand contest, but then she went on and explained: "When God threw us out of Eden, He sent down a lot of bugs to live with us. That was part of His way to keep reminding us that we'd had this falling out with Him and we were going to have to live down here with bugs forever."

I wasn't sure about Emily Lou's theology, but it made a lot of sense to me back then. And I just accepted bugs as a tradeoff for where I lived.

But now that I have been in Florida for twenty years, I am beginning to think about bugs in a whole new way. I know that when I was getting on the plane to head back from California, I could hardly wait to get home to my bugs. I live on a dirt road back in thick Florida woods, and one of my greatest treats is to sit out on my screened porch in late May and watch the fireflies light up the woods like dancing strings of Christmas lights.

In summer the cicadas take over, unseen but heard, tuning up a whole jazz band in the woods in the hot afternoons. They play sets late into the night, then take the morning off like most hard working musicians. And I know that they are due their rest. For I can't listen to them without marveling that each one has spent up to seventeen years underground waiting for this chance to sing.

If a cricket happens to get into my house, I take it as a compliment. I figure he's seeing the worst of my housekeeping, down there near the floorboards in hidden spots, and yet his sounds don't ever sound irritated or put out with me in the least for all the dust he sees. No, I couldn't live without my bug musicians. And as for frogs? Oh, don't get me started on my frogs.

It's quite clear, though, I'm not cut out for paradise. Not now, if ever. If you want to know the truth, I think the silence would really bug me.

Cat

It's funny what the kids leave you when they move out. Like my son's cat. He bought her outside of the mall for five dollars. This didn't make a bit of sense. We already had two cats, one a male and one fixed. But he said she was a bargain, and it was the last thing he'd ever ask me for. The naked truth is he was eleven, in the first throws of pre-puberty and had a veiled need to watch something have babies.

We named her Big Mama and set about waiting for her to grow up and get ready. But when she was nearly a year old, we were disheartened with the news of learning she was wired weird. Her brain would fire off the command 'attack' at any old time for no good reason, so she would sink her teeth into whatever moved, which was usually some part of a human. She would then have to be pried loose. More than once at dinner parties, and at other sorts of get-togethers, we'd wag her from the end of a sock just to display what she was really made of. But still we felt an obligation to stop the end of her line. She was quickly spayed, but continued to live happily on and on and on. And most often now on the top of my computer.

Big Mama lies up there like a black and white shirt my son has taken off and thrown, so she has landed half on, half off, and with a good bit hanging down.

Sometimes I work right through her naps, reading my sentences in between her toes and tail, which she moves across the screen like a car's windshield wiper set on real, real slow.

Last winter I made the mistake of inviting a stray dog in — after all, it was one of those rare Florida nights when it was going to dip down below freezing, and the dog was standing outside my back door looking real old and pitiful. I locked him in the utility room and then went to bed under my own electric blanket.

Somehow during the night, the old, cold dog got loose in the house. He helped himself to a midnight snack in the kitchen, and for most of the rest of the night he held Big Mama hostage on top of my computer — where, of course, she really didn't mind staying. (And he didn't realize, either, just exactly whom he was dealing with.) But apparently the dog was her excuse for not getting up and going to her cat box as she knew she should.

The next morning when I opened the front door and let the old dog go on his way, and I turned on my computer, it made a sound like a car crash. I guess some smarty-pants computer engineer somewhere thought it would be real funny to program a computer to make this sound when your computer has crashed and burned. It took me awhile, though, to figure out that what was streaked down my monitor's screen was not orange juice.

I called the 1-800 number for the Computer's Troubleshooters. I couldn't lie. But I also knew that if I told the truth, there'd be no way anybody would replace or fix my computer. Nothing about a cat was mentioned in the warranty; I'd already studied that hard. But when some guy named Herb answered, and I truthfully told him what my cat had done, I asked anyway, "Do you think this could be considered an act of God?"

This story about my cat and the computer was apparently so funny to computer troubleshooters and engineers everywhere that the news of it flew between them fast, and the company fixed my computer pronto, and at a minimum charge. But now I can't go into a computer store for so much as a new disk but that when I whip out my Visa with my name on it, I get asked, "Aren't you that lady with that cat who...." which is then followed by a discreet pause, then a few seconds while they laugh themselves silly.

I guess there're worse reasons for getting passed around on the internet.

Big Mama still sleeps on top of my monitor, but I cover the computer's brains with plastic wrap now, just in case. And occasionally she moves down to the keyboard, where, when my head is lowered in deep thought, she puts her paw on the keyboard and shoots a whole page of zeros across the screen.

I'm not sure if Big Mama wants a computer for herself, or if she's sending e-mail to her own kind.

Frankly, I'm scared to ask.

OOOO OOO:

OOOOOOO OOOOOO OOOOO OOOOOOOO OOOOOOO OOOOOOOOOO. OOOOOOOOOO OOOO OOO OO OOO OOOOO OOOOOOOOOOOO OOOOOOOOOO OOOOOOO OO OOO OOOOOOOOO OOOOO. OOOOOOOO OOOO OOOOOOOOO OOOOOOO OOOOOOO. OOOOOOOOOOOOOOOOOOOOOOOOOOOO.

OOOOO,

OOO

Ants

Recently I was feeling pretty smug about being a human. What started all of this was looking around my office and seeing how hooked up I am. I have the latest computer, my own e-mail address, my own fax machine, my own voice mail, my own cellular telephone. Yep, I'm not ever out of reach of anybody. And now almost nothing can happen anywhere that I can't find out about it, if I really want to.

My cat though — the one my son bought at a horse show for two dollars — is not impressed. I'll admit, I've never expected much out of a two- dollar cat, but that doesn't stop him from expecting a lot of me. He likes his food on the floor. I'm not talking about in a bowl, either. When I say he likes his food on the floor, I mean just that, slap flat on the tile floor. He uses his paw to lift it out of the bowl and set it on the floor before he will eat it, too. And he craves tuna. But I'll be darned if I'll be owned by a two-dollar cat. So I simply refuse to put his tuna straight on the floor. I let him pick it out of his bowl himself.

I never was any good at getting my kids to clean up after themselves, so I know better than to even try with this cat. The trouble is, last week I got lazy and just didn't wipe up my cat's tuna crumbs right after his breakfast. I left his mess on the tile a couple of hours. And in those couple of hours something happened that made me know we humans aren't what we're cracked up to be. Because somehow one ant got into my house and then got on the ant internet and put out the word that I was serving free tuna.

By the time I was ready to clean up my cat's mess, there were a couple of hundred ants having a tuna convention in my kitchen, swapping recipes and backpacking crumbs up the wall and onto the window sills and out into the yard and across the pasture and down the street.

Over the next few days, I did terrible things to these ants, from an ant's point of view. And yet not so terrible things from a human's point of view. I sprayed them and swept them and vacuumed them up. I even mopped. That's when I tried to drown them out. Then I put down a slick blue place mat for the cat to eat off of. But it didn't matter. I swear those ants could hear me opening a can of tuna all the way down to Tampa. And they really seemed to like that place mat.

Whatever signal they were sending to get in touch with each other was far faster and more efficient than anything I'd seen. No doubt they were setting up chat rooms and web pages like crazy. And I started having nightmares that I was listed somewhere on an ant's internet as 'The Tuna Lady.'

I'd like to say that the result of all this was something real logical and admirable — like I stopped serving tuna. Or I got rid of the cat. Or I called a bug man to exterminate my house. But I think I just got so impressed with the ants' communication system that I stopped doing anything.

Now I put the cat's food straight on the floor, and I sit and watch for the ants. If I can just find out some way to communicate with them, I'm going to get the secret to their software and sell it on the internet.

Space

Living here in North Central Florida we have a special challenge, which is really an honor, and that's to not let our bodily functions go bananas when the space shuttle comes in for a landing. Living on the space shuttle's landing path takes a special calm. And every time I hear that boom and my house shakes and my cats jump into the air and hightail it under the bed, I think about that story of Chicken Little and how his hysterical personality led him to broadcast throughout his neighborhood that the sky was falling.

When I was a little kid, I hated Chicken Little. I just had no patience for anybody, much less a chicken, who could not handle the little ups and downs of life — especially getting hit on the head by a falling nut which then led him to use deductive reasoning to figure out that the sky was falling. Now, I'm going to say this again: I hated Chicken Little. And he has nothing to do with how I acted a couple of years ago when I heard this boom that made me jump out of my skin, followed by my house shaking and my cats going bananas under my bed and my dog hiding in the shower so she could privately have a five minute, but full-fledged, nervous breakdown. I just calmly called my neighbor and asked her if a sink hole had opened up anywhere that she could see.

I'd read about those sink holes — how they could appear like a yawn in the middle of a road and swallow a whole line of five o'clock traffic. Or how they could just suck down a house like my Uncle Bill likes to show off when he eats Jalapenos. I got out maps and looked at just exactly where my house was sitting. But you know, you can't believe everything those maps tell you. I thought it was probably a good idea for the next few months to sleep hanging onto the bed posts, so if I did get sucked down into a sinkhole in the middle of REM sleep, I at least wouldn't be the first thing to hit the bottom.

Over those next few years, as I heard more and more booms and my house never sank, I got to feeling pretty smug. I didn't get used to the bangs or the house shaking, but I did get smug. Then one day when I mentioned to my neighbor that we must just be living on an inactive sink hole, (like one of those inactive volcanoes that look mean and spit smoke but are about as dangerous as a stuffed snake), she asked me what made me think we were on a sink hole in the first place?

"Those booms," I said. "And doesn't your house shake?"

"Well, yes," she told me, "but that's just the Space Shuttle going over." She also explained that you could read in the newspaper when it was expected to be coming in for a landing, and you could be prepared, if you wanted to be.

Well, now I don't know how in the world you can get prepared for your house shaking and your cats going bananas and your dog acting pitiful. But I've tried. I take the newspaper and read it to them. I explain that they are living in the space age and that they are being challenged by a space shuttle to just keep their feet on the ground when it lands. Then I tell them the story of that stupid Chicken Little who misread the sky, and I remind them we are not at all like him. Not at all.

Sunshine

Florida isn't called "The Sunshine State" for nothing. When I moved here twenty years ago, I'm sure I was suffering from that S.A.D. disease. I know its initials stand for something like Sunlight Affective Disorder, but to me it makes more sense to think of it as Sourpuss-and-Down-in-the-Mouth-Disease.

Back where I lived in places where the winters were long, a lot of people had it and most especially those who answered telephones and pumped gas and sold you groceries and drove cars. In five o'clock traffic, someone behind the wheel with Sourpuss-and-Down-in-the-Mouth-Disease would just as soon cut you out of a lane as look at you. As for answering a telephone, well, let's just say that what they said and how they said it was protected best of all by the fact that they were talking over a whole lot of wires and at a distance, since if you could reach them, you'd punch out their lights.

But here in Florida where we have more sunlight year round than we can soak in, we're pretty perky — at least until the humidity wilts us, and then we just tend to jump into some water somewhere, or sit in the shade, or go inside into the air conditioning and call someone on the telephone. I think it's all the sweat in our eyes that makes for a good number of wrong number calls, or maybe it's that the humidity has gotten to us so much that taking off our sunglasses to dial the right numbers requires too much effort, so we just punch or dial whatever looks close.

I know it sounds crazy, but I enjoy these wrong number calls, because usually they go something like this:

"Hello." I say.

"Hello." Someone says back. And then, "Martha?"

"There's no Martha here."

"Oh, really? I was calling my Aunt Martha at 555-4545."

"Well, this is 554-5555."

"Oh! I should have known that the minute you said 'Hello'. You don't sound a thing like Aunt Martha. Where did you move here from?"

When I tell them, they usually know someone who lived there, too, or at least close. Then I learn a good bit about Aunt Martha, and they learn a good bit about me, if I want to tell them. And neither of us is the least bit put out by the fact that we got in touch on a fluke, or that if we drove past each other in five o'clock traffic, we wouldn't even recognize that fact.

Sometimes when I get a wrong number, we do nothing but talk about the weather. If it's too hot, we complain. If it's too dry, we worry together. We know we can't do anything about the weather, but we wouldn't want to trade it, either — not really.

This is the only place I know where most people with Sourpuss-and-Down-in-the-Mouth-Disease can get over it enough to become good conversationalists to someone whom they will never even meet. It's the only place I know where someone will sit back and enjoy a mistake, and where recovery can be contagious.

Sunsets

I guess I'd never really seen a sunset until I moved to Florida. I didn't understand how the sun's disappearance could be considered a whole show, like it is in Key West, where every day at dusk people gather on the dock to clap at the exact moment when the sun slips below the horizon, like a diva twirling behind the curtain with a wink and a smile. I didn't know, either, how the sun can take over the whole sky in a paint show as it does at Cedar Key, where it lingers on the water of the Gulf like a glowing basketball that, in one swift second, is slam dunked to Australia. But it is only on the farm where I live now, when in early July at 7:00 P.M. as the sun perches on the top of the tree line on the western side of the big pasture, that I hear it sing.

Like the opening notes of *Old Man River*, it starts a low humming near the end of supper, at just about the time I am doing the dishes, or stacking them up to wait until morning. So at 8:00, I move out onto the front porch to sit in a wicker chair and position myself behind one of the house columns. This is the only way my eyes will allow me to see what seems like a swollen egg yolk hanging at arm's length on the horizon with a fierceness that defies a direct look. Its intensity is as straight-on as a rap singer doing an in-your-face rhyme. On either side of the column, I watch long streaks of pink bleed into the clouds and a dark V of birds fly in formation across them, then separate into single songs that land in the trees near where I am.

Every once in a while I peek around the column for a direct eye-hit at the sun, which only sharply tells me, Not yet; it is still too soon to gaze at it, one-on-one. Clouds begin to form across it like wrinkles in a cotton sheet.

At 8:10, it is as if a peach has exploded in a hallelujah of juice that begins dripping on someone's shirt front, and in another five minutes the air begins to feel cool. The clouds spread across the sky in a strong shade of lavender; and the cicadas and crickets come out in full force, their voices like backup singers for the diva who is about to exit.

By 8:20, I can steal short views of the sun without having to look away. It is a half circle by then, similar to a quarter slipping into a coin slot. As it sinks, it loses its shape and becomes only its essence, a hole in the sky where a fire is lit. I lean all the way around the column because I can steadily watch now without turning away. The clouds are busy sewing the openings shut, so that by 8:25 it seems that a rag has just wiped up the spilled juice, leaving only muted stains of orange and pink.

Tonight the clouds have formed a 7 in a river of orange that takes a sharp left turn and flows into a bank of trees that line the sky at the edge of the pasture. There is a blueberry grayness to the light that lingers for a long time after the sun has left, leaving me with the sound of my bugs and the smell of jasmine. Somewhere near the edge of the porch a bullfrog croaks as if someone is banging on a hollow pipe.

The poet John Greenleaf Whittier wrote that beauty seen is never lost. That God's colors all are fast. Oscar Wilde said that nobody of any real culture ever talks about the beauty of sunset, that sunsets are quite old fashioned and to admire them is a distinct sign of provincialism of temperament. He also added that on the other hand, they go on.

I know that it is written down in lots of places that we who live on the earth are spinning at 1,000 miles an hour, circling the sun at one hundred thousand miles an hour, and together hurling through space in our galaxy of The Milky Way at a speed of one-hundred thousand miles a second. But these facts are hard for me even to imagine. All I can really believe is that the sun never leaves us, and we never leave it. And so every night after supper, I go out to wave to the sun as I once did to my kids when they were just taking a quick turn on their bikes around the block. I am also tempted to answer its song with a few bars of a lullaby, for the habits of mothers tend to go on, too.

Yes, calling home a place where the sunsets are spectacular is one fine way to end the day.

Hurricanes

Hurricanes are like skunks — the farther away from them you are, the better. Yet no one can live in Florida for very long without occasionally getting sideswiped by one. So, we squirrel away water in bottles, candles galore and food guaranteed not to rot.

It was when the tropical storm Josephine thought about changing her mind and becoming a full-fledged hurricane and heading into Cedar Key (as though she'd heard there was a 50% - Off Sale on everything in the whole town) that I was forced to become up close and personal with her.

I was vacationing in Cedar Key with my dog and three cats. At first I didn't think anything about Josephine heading toward us, but when somebody on the TV weather channel stood up and said Josephine was on her way to becoming a bonafide hurricane with her eye on Cedar Key, I freaked out. Underneath my bedroom window, it looked like Josephine was putting the water of the Gulf of Mexico into a drink mixer and was dead-set on turning it on high.

All I could think about was her coming at my townhouse, and cat fur flying everywhere. Visions of water all the way through the first floor sent me and my dog into high gear. Neither of us is a good swimmer; she doesn't even like baths. Just the sound of thunder sends her into my closet to bury her head in my shoes. So we started picking and choosing what we could sacrifice and what we couldn't — which is an interesting exercise in itself. I chose my computer over my wardrobe, and my dog chose to sit in the car over everything.

Like a good fireman, I went back into my house and hunted down each cat one at a time and carried them through the blustery wind to the car. Seeing the Cedar Key Islanders go into high gear was like watching a well-rehearsed dance. They moved boats out of the angry water with thick life vests on and drove their cars to park them on the highest ground in town. They would never evacuate, they said. The last time they had done that, their town had been looted.

They are a strong tight band, these Cedar Key Islanders, and I felt pretty guilty about driving off and leaving them there. But after all, I had my cats to think about, and my dog was riding shotgun with a look on her face that said if I didn't step on it, she was going to have a full-fledged public nervous breakdown. I drove the fifty miles of blacktop road as if I were the lead rider in a posse, and the whole way, one cat sat on my head, while the dog fogged up the windows with her panting. I pulled into a hotel whose marquee said it welcomed evacuees, but when the night manager saw my dog, he hung a sign on my door that said to skip the maid service.

A day later when I returned to Cedar Key, Josephine was headed to the Panhandle. She'd never developed into a full-blown hurricane, and she'd never hit Cedar Key full force with her eye, either. But she caused a mess, all the same.

The sky was blue, and the clouds swirled through it with the dreamy look of wedding clothes. The roads were strewn with sea weed, mud and bits of broken piers. The islanders were sweeping it all up into piles, readying it for cleaning trucks to haul away. The stores opened their doors and moved their wet parts out into the streets to dry. People swept the walks and curbs and calmly put their houses back in order.

I moved my cats and dog back into my townhouse, hosed out the air conditioner, then sat down to look out through my salt-stained windows at the Gulf. It was calm and beautiful and clearly lying through its teeth about ever having stepped over the sea walls and beaches to run over the town. It reminded me of an angelic toddler who, the day before, had wrecked my house, which makes me know that all this discussion about naming hurricanes after women, then throwing in a few men's names just to equal things up isn't even close to getting it right. They should instead take on the names of two-year-olds. Maybe something like Mikey, and Suzy or Kimmy and Chip — and very definitely, Josie.

It's preparing for them though that made all of us down here in Florida ready way ahead of everybody when all the hoopla started about the new century. Yeah, we breezed right through Y2K.

Perfect Gift

Yesterday I saw a child receive the perfect gift. I didn't expect to see it. He didn't expect to receive it. And it happened in the most unlikely place. It was on the airplane flying back from the horse show in Oklahoma. I was sitting beside this eight-year-old boy and his mother. Just as we started to come in for a landing, the heavens let loose with one of those gullywhopper thunderstorms. Lightning, rain, thunder — you know the kind — so you start wishing the stewardess would get up and start serving drinks again. You begin to wonder, too, if your affairs are enough in order to keep all your relatives from squabbling over whatever piddling stuff you leave.

We bounced around for a while, like one of those carnival rides I never had enough guts to buy a ticket for. Then the pilot came on over the microphone and said in his smooth-as-chewing-gum voice that it was just way too rough for him to try to set us down here, so he was just going to head on over to Jacksonville and set us down there.

As soon as we flew out of the bad weather, and the plane stopped bucking, a low moan of complaint moved throughout the coach section. Not only did we now face another thirty minute plane ride, but our relatives or friends, who had come to meet us, were standing down there on the ground being told we were a no-show. The plan was that a bus was being sent to pick us up at the other airport, then we'd have to ride it all the way back.

The boy sitting beside me was dressed in jeans and boots and a plaid shirt. He had a cowlick over his forehead like a hand of cards, and his mother was in shorts with a ruffled blouse. They reminded me of people I had grown up with in the cotton belt in Arkansas. More than likely their lives moved to the rhythm of weather and crops, or maybe night shifts and overtime. When I asked them who would have been waiting for them, I learned that the boy's father had driven fifty miles to be at the airport. Our delay was a real bummer, we agreed. And the mother was a good bit distressed. It was then that the most amazing exchange took place.

While the rest of us ducked back into our magazines, or went on with grumbling about our inconvenience, the boy began telling his mother stories. I don't know what they were about, or where he got them; but looking at his mother's face you would have thought he was telling her the most wonderful and hilarious tales she'd ever heard. She was laughing and watching him as if his every third sentence held the most delicious surprise. More than once, she reached over and punched him on his arm and cried out, "Stop, stop. I can't take it anymore," as if she were someone being tickled to death. The more she teasingly punched him, the more he talked on.

Throughout our whole ride, and even after we were taxiing down the runway into our detoured airport, the boy and his mother continued their interchange. When I got up to get my bag out of the overhead compartment, I glanced down at them. They weren't even aware that I'd been watching them. But the boy's mother was still listening, and I could see that without a doubt the most wondrous light had been lit in that boy's face.

I'm pretty sure it's still there. In fact, I'm pretty convinced that if anything lasts at all, it is this kind of light that is eternal.

I consider it a privilege to have been there when it was given.

Christmas Gifts

We have a rule in our family that you can't give as a Christmas gift something you once got as a gift yourself, and didn't like, until a decade has passed. This is called a ten-year re-gifting cycle, and it works on the premise that nobody in our family has a memory that will hold a fact in it for longer than ten years. So if you gave Uncle Bill a green fishing hat with embroidered turtles on it one year and it boomerangs back to you on Christmas day ten years later, it will look only familiar. In fact, you will wonder how in the world did Uncle Bill know your taste so well?

This theory, of course, rests on a well-known premise: that the best way to pick out a gift is to choose something you yourself like and would want. So for many years now, we have followed this rule of picking out a gift, feeling certain that because we ourselves have liked it, the person we are giving it to is sure to love it as well. But I hate to tell you this: it just ain't so.

Uncle Bill hated green, and he especially didn't want anything with turtles embroidered on it. I don't know why, it was just something inside of him that the idea of wearing a turtle set off. None of us knew this until after he died, when we found a whole trunk load of unworn clothes with turtles on them. And my Aunt Betty Lou—she despised little Bo Peep statues, and yet her husband gave her one every Christmas for the fifty years they were married. He thought they were the cutest things in the world and just assumed she would think so, too. We never learned how much she disliked them until we read her will in which she instructed us to send all those Bo Peep statues straight to Hell.

Of course, if I hadn't been raised in such a polite family, none of this would be a problem. We could just open our gifts on Christmas morning and tell each other that what we've been given is the ugliest, stupidest thing we've ever seen, and to take it back pronto and give us the money instead so we can go out and get what we really want. But doing this somehow does something to ruin your taste for Christmas dinner. And there's something, too, about giving just money that seems cold, calculating, lazy, and as impersonal as a recorded message.

So this year, I've wracked my brain and come up with a new tradition. It is based on honesty, and yet it won't ruin anybody's dinner. Better yet, it is bound to make everybody happy. Because my plan is to give what you really want and then swap right away. It's going to be a little unusual, but in the long run I think it'll be okay. I just hope my husband remembers the new plan when he opens his box of diamond earrings. I'm pretty sure he will, though, because I've already scratched a corner of the paper off my gift and seen the words, 10-in. compound miter saw with dust bag.

This is the year I think we're going to get the gifts that right away keep on giving.

Sawed-off Santa

It was 9:43 A.M. The headmistress's voice sounded desperate. "Don Hern has the flu." It was the year my son was in the fifth grade. Why I got the call I can only speculate. "Don was going to play Santa for us today," she explained. "Do you have any ideas?"

I guess word had gotten around that I owned a Santa suit, a sixty-five dollar job ordered the year before from the Sears Catalog. I had worn it on the past Halloween and had nearly died from heat exhaustion while in it. Or, maybe the head mistress knew I would be home at 9:43 with not much on my mind but writing a novel. I went through my list of available men. Plumbers, pool cleaners, roofers — the ones whose mobile phone numbers I knew by heart. But as I was halfway through the list, she blurted out: "Will you do it?"

"Oh, I don't know," I said. "I'm not really built for it. Right off, the kids will know I'm a fake."

What I was thinking about was Don Hern — six feet two, three hundred pounds with a nickname of Slim. I'm five-foot-three on a good day. And on that last Halloween when I'd been in the Santa suit, a middle school kid had told me I looked gay.

"But we're desperate," she said. She then went on and painted a pitiful picture — the four-year old class of pre-kindergartners already lining up at the play yard gate because they'd been told that after recess Santa was going to visit.

Damn. Nothing gets to me quite like little kids' hope. "Give me forty-five minutes," I said.

When I walked out the door and headed for the station wagon, the dog didn't ask to go. I knew she knew it was me. Under the fake beard and eyebrows and the pillow-stuffed suit, we could both still smell my riding boots. I thought they'd lend an air of authenticity. After all, working around reindeer and horses couldn't be all that different. But when the dog didn't ask to go, I got nervous. She's rarely ever too embarrassed to be seen with me in public.

Driving a station wagon dressed in a Santa suit was like being an Orange Bowl queen on a float. So many honks and waves made the going tough, so when I pulled up in front of the school, I was even later than I'd promised. At sight of me, the kids on the playground whipped themselves into a frenzy. The playground teacher kept blowing her whistle and telling them to line up and calm down. When they did — that's when I got stage fright.

How in the world was I going to satisfy these little ones? My son's class didn't worry me. I knew I could count on them to go along with me as just a game. But these little four and five year olds — they had set ideas about Santa. Even with manure on my boots, I knew I could raise doubts in their minds that could haunt them forever. I could get calls from their parents. I might even be accused of ruining their Christmas.

If I hadn't seen the headmistress at the door waving me in, I wouldn't have made it. I followed her down the hall, then stopped off at the Girls' Bathroom for one more stomach lift.

As I was pulling at things and hand combing my mustache, two little girls came out of the same stall door behind me and looked at my backside. I could see them in the mirror over the sinks. They had on miniskirts, and one had a ponytail coming out of the top of her head. I figured they were about in the second grade. The tallest one met my eyes in the mirror and asked, "You're going to visit in our class today, aren't you?"

I was reluctant to try out my Santa Claus voice, so I nodded.

"Well, I want to qualify her," she said and pointed to her side-kick. "She's been good all year."

Qualify. The word smacked of testing. It reminded me of applications and of a society quick to rank people. I remembered the old stories about Santa Claus and Christmas and that he came to only those children who'd been good all year. When I was growing up, it was said that if you weren't good you'd get switches and ashes or coal in your stocking instead of toys. Yet all the years I'd been raising my own children and entertaining their friends, I hadn't met one kid who was not good. In fact, I don't believe that kids aren't good. They're all good, good to the last drop. Good to go. Good as good gets. From time to time, they might do things that aren't all that hot, but that doesn't mean a whole hill of beans next the value of the kids themselves.

"I'll remember that," I said, going out of the bathroom into the hall. That's when I realized I had the handle I needed to pull off the day.

In the pre-kindergarten room, as the first child came to sit on my lap, I looked down at the rest of the class sitting on the floor around us and asked, "Who'll vouch for him?" When they all looked blank, I explained, "Who'll stand up and say he's been good all year? — that's what vouch means."

All twenty-five kids jumped to their feet. They did it, too, for every kid in the room, just stood up, over and over, until everyone

Thanksgiving Peas

On Thanksgiving when I was nine years old and growing up in a little cotton town in Arkansas, my mother decided to have a showdown over peas. I didn't like them, and I didn't see any reason to start to. It's English peas I'm talking about. Black-eyed I got along with. But the little green ones that were the color of frogs left me cold.

"Go ahead, eat 'em," she said, spooning them onto my plate so they rolled into the turkey. I pressed my lips together tight as a child-safe cap on aspirin. Nary a pea would pass down my throat I declared.

"Well," my mother said. "We'll just all sit here until they do, then." In truth, I know what she was worried about. I was skinny and pale and frequently called Bean Pole, and, bless-her-heart, Mama thought that somehow eating peas would improve me.

While I stared at my mound of them, I, in turn, got stared at by my brother, my father, my Great Aunt Gladys, my Great Uncle Bubba and six cousins five times removed. After a while, I started feeling pretty guilty about keeping them from dessert. So with a straight-eyed look wired right into the eyeballs of my mother, I ate the peas she had put on my plate and then, for spite, reached over and drank the rest of the whole bowl. When I looked up, everybody started clapping, and pumpkin pie was served.

While the adults went out to sit on the porch, we kids headed to the water tower for a game of football. Pretty soon the whole neighborhood was there.

My brother was the captain of one team, and as usual he didn't want any girls on his side, and especially me. The other team didn't want me, either. Even after a turkey dinner and a whole bowl of peas, I was considered to be too light for the job.

But I was good at pestering. And finally, "All right," my brother said, "you can play— IF you block Joe Wompler." Nobody else wanted to. Joe Wompler was one of those twelve-year-old kids who had the body of a man before he even had chest hair. He would later go on to become a star guard for the Razorbacks, but now he was twelve and weighing a whole turkey dinner more.

I lined up, head to head with Joe, his face the size of an uncut pie just opposite mine. The last things I heard were the sounds of the football snapping into my brother's hands and then the dull thump of Joe Wompler landing on my head. While I was coming to, my brother started pleading, "Please don't tell Mama. You're not going to tell Mama, are you?"

He guided me all the way home, since I was knocked drunk as a skunk. And still, he kept coaching me, "And you're not going to tell Daddy, either, are you?"

I must admit, the smell of guilt coming from him was rather sweet and real noticeable. He escorted me across the front porch and into the living room, where I promptly lost my peas.

That night as I went to bed, my mother came to lean over me. "I didn't mean to make you sick, forcing you to eat all that," she said. "I won't do it again. Especially in front of a whole lot of people like today."

I knew I should tell her the truth about the football game and that I'd pestered my brother to let me play in the first place and that my getting sick hadn't been her fault at all. But I didn't. Instead I just lay there and thought about how wonderful guilt is. How it can make all of us stop and look at each other and even ourselves.

I've lived with the guilt of that silence for more than forty years. I think I'll call the kids and tell them.

The Flu

Why is it that when the flu bug hits my house, it becomes a point of celebration if I lose my voice. If 'The Mama' is vocally put out of commission, it seems that everybody picks up a pen and starts writing their own book called, "BAD AS I WANNA BE." My silence is more than golden, it's permission.

When I stand up out of my sick bed to suck a lemon or any of those other remedies for laryngitis, I can catch sight of my family dancing in the halls. I know that it is only the delirium of my fever that makes me see that scene in the *Wizard of Oz* when Dorothy and her friends cavort around singing, *Ding Dong, the Witch is Dead.*

I'm not saying that I have bad children or that I am mistreated or that I am occasionally referred to as a witch — oh no — it's just that the role of being 'The Mama' frequently carries with it the popularity of a three-day old fish. Clearly, the job is no small potatoes. It's no piece of cake either, and I have yet to come up with a dish to describe it, unless it's trying to find a recipe for gizzards or praying to God that your turkey gravy will thicken.

Probably only the President of the United States understands what exercising veto powers can take out of you. Frequently throughout the day I sing, *Nobody Knows the Trouble I've Seen*, and in moments when I'm not even dizzy with the flu, I see Father Time staring at me and shaking his head, and asking, "If you don't pass on civilization, who the heck is goin' to?" Somehow I know he isn't referring to just the act of physical birth, which is what really scares me. You can get put to sleep through most of that.

When the flu hits and I lose my voice, somewhere along about the second day, I start writing notes. I get the kind with the little sticky backs so I can crawl around the house and stick them to the places that need the most immediate attention, like the dog, on which I write, "Feed Me." And the milk, on which rides the reminder, "Put On My Top." I heap yards of dirty clothes on the lid of the washing machine and affix the words, "Put me in, Turn me on, Pull me out, and Put me on." I lie down on the floor and scoot up behind the TV and pull out from it a bunch of wadded notes with school letterheads, that all say, "Have your mother call me." I press them out with a rolling pin and tape them onto the TV screen with the warning: "Don't lie about this. Call your teacher right his minute and say that as soon as your mother can speak, she's dialing your number."

I'm on to that old trick, too, about when my notes are left unread because my handwriting is said to be too messy, or that clearly my fever has clouded my judgment. I'm no dummy, I know how to use e-mail. I can type and fashion letters out of noodles. No, having the flu and losing my voice is never for me just having the flu and losing my voice. It's a special challenge to my creative powers.

Now that my kids are grown and have moved on into their own lives, they still relish my silence when I have the flu. I call them up, though, and let them do the talking. Funny thing, how they never seem to hear my words coming out of their mouths.

I'm pretty sure that means I've put in my two cents worth toward passing on civilization.

Luck

There's this old saying about the luck of the Irish. Having good luck is nothing to sneeze at. And for a long time, I've wondered how to get some of it for myself.

For a while I thought the fact that the Irish are lucky had something to do with their blarney stone. Because the legend goes that if a person kisses it, he will be given the gift of gab, which I think means he can talk his way out of anything. I've seen that blarney stone. It's set at the top of a wall of a fifteenth century castle, and you have to lie down on your back, have some man hold your feet so you won't go flying out backwards down a cliff while you arch back to kiss the stone which is behind your head.

I watched a whole line of people lie back and kiss that stone, but I'm afraid of heights, and I never had the guts to do it myself. I didn't like the fact that I'd be way up in the air while I was kissing it, and that while I was doing it some stranger would be holding my feet. With my luck, I figured he'd let go, and that would be that. Silenced forever.

When the Irish first came to this country, they did so mainly because their potato crop had failed and they were in danger of starving. The first jobs they had here were connecting parts of our country by building canals like the Erie and the Susquehanna. They were called the pick-and-shovel Irish, and I imagine the whole time they were picking and shoveling they were talking like mad and winning horse races and crap games and door prizes at Spaghetti Suppers.

I've got some Irish blood in me, too, but apparently not enough to make me lucky. In fact, it's hard to get my friends to go anywhere with me. For on the way, it is likely that I'll have a flat tire. And when we stop for lunch and head on into the Waffle House, I usually step in gum. As I go into the bathroom to try to get it off, the doorknob often comes off in my hands.

People tend to say, "You make your own luck." But I know deep down I have done nothing to cause this, except maybe by not having enough Irish in me.

I'm not saying, either, that I'm not blessed. Oh no. In the big things, the things that really count, like the fact that my overall general health is more than good and that I have given easy birth to two fine children with all their necessary parts, I am way ahead. And I wouldn't trade.

I am a little jealous, though. I have a friend who is three-fourth's Irish, and she can buy a lottery ticket and win at least five dollars just by filling in a few dots with a pencil. She gets a parking space anywhere she goes. And last week she won a dog at a Spaghetti Supper.

I resent, too, that luck is called a lady. Oh, I know where that little saying comes from. Some man made it up to explain how fickle we women are. But my lack of luck never seems to leave. And I've never known a lady, either, to cause as much of a mess as the one that is following me.

Whenever I think I'd like to trade places with my lucky friend, I usually change my mind. Because in the final analysis, I'd much rather be blessed than lucky. And when I was sitting beside her at that Spaghetti Supper last week, I knew the last thing I really needed was that dog.

The Blues

Every once in a while I get the low-down, hang-dog, gut-bucket blues — if you know what I mean. When this happens, it seems the whole planet is just too mean to live on. I see too clearly how it is a dog-eat-dog world, and yet I have never met a human who had anywhere near the capacity for unconditional love that a dog has.

Oh, I could stay down there in the compost pile of my soul's sewer for nigh on for the rest of my life, I guess. But sooner or later I resort to two things, which never seem to fail in getting me back out into the world and passing for being sweet and talking nice, at least 50 percent of the time.

First, I go out onto my front porch and cut the pee-doodle squat out of the plant that is sitting beside my wicker chair. I don't know what kind of a plant it is, but it is not a weed. It is something kin to a hot house flower, I think, which means that it is not bred to take abuse. And yet I pretty nearly clip the stuffings out of every part of it, so that if it were a human I would have rendered it too ugly for eyes. I then set it out in the sun and fail to give it a drink of any kind, unless I just happen to walk by with a half empty glass of Pepsi and decide to share it. The idea is to let that plant take its chances. Let's just see how the elements treat it, I think. And then, "Ah-ha," I say to my plant — with no intention to talk nice. "You'll see: this is not a kind world. You won't make it, not this time, not this time."

And then it does, and I have to eat my words and move the blooming plant back up to its usual place beside my wicker chair where, every time I sit down beside it I half expect it to remind me what a hard-hearted kick-butt sort of person I am. But it is silent and forgiving. Yeah, it's quite a plant.

The other thing I do — and now I know this is going to sound even crazier than trying to murder a plant — I drive around Gainesville. I've been doing it for twenty years now, and the first time I did, I just couldn't get over how I could gesture through my windshield to ask someone to let me into their lane, and they did. They actually nodded their head, made eye-to-eye contact through two windshields, and held back their horse power to make a space for me. I have never lived anywhere where this happens — and I have lived a lot of places and driven down a lot of roads.

Our streets are so narrow, we have to cooperate or no one would get anywhere. But I suspect, too, that our sense of niceness is contagious, so that if you move here as a motor-revving, horn-honking hard heart, you're going to stand out, and it's not going to be pretty. For instance, consider that right hand turn on red. I once got honked at for not taking it. I figure it's one of the last things we can do, sit there at a light and think, "Do I really want to go right on red if I get a chance?" It's not like when the light turns green and you know you gotta go. No. Right on red should be left to a person's discretion. But when I got honked at, everybody drove past the honker and stared at him through his windshield until he wilted like the plant on my porch never will. I guess our silently agreed upon driving etiquette weeds out the big honkers who think they have to get somewhere in two minutes or die trying.

What's got me worried now, though, is that if we widen all our roads and speed up, are we going to change?

Boy, I sure hope not, because if we do, I'm going to have to get two of those plants to abuse. And for the life of me, I can't remember where I got the first one.

A Slipping Down Personality

This year as I was thinking about making my New Year's Resolutions, I discovered something very new. It appears that over the last year I have gone straight from being an A Personality to a C — skipped B altogether.

Used to, I didn't even have to have an alarm clock. My body was set on Go, and I would just wake up and do whatever needed to be done. I arrived early everywhere and was always the first in line. But now, I sleep till the sun is well up. I arrive fashionably late everywhere, and if I haven't changed my sheets in over a week, I don't even notice.

In fact, if the cat sleeps with me, (the $2 one), I just roll over on top of him now and keep on snoring. Used to be, the idea of him in the bed with me would send me hunting up the broom to scare him out and then sweep up whatever dander he left. When we first got this cat, my son named him Big Shooter, but lately neither Big Shooter nor I seem very interested in doing anything big. I think he's given up altogether being a nocturnal animal and prowling while the moon is up. And if I prowl at all, it is mostly between two and four in the afternoon. Neither one of us seems very interested in setting the world on fire or catching a mouse.

I've noticed, too, that if I'm having a bad hair day, it still looks pretty good to me. And if I have a run in my stocking, I just let it run, whereas I used to twist it around so it wouldn't show, or do something really amazing like paint nail polish on it so it wouldn't run any farther. In fact, if you're going to have a run in your stocking, seems to me it's a good idea to let it be a whopper. But the biggest point of this is that now I rarely even wear stockings. Tennis shoes and jeans seem to go just about everywhere.

I eat day-old donuts and read day-old newspapers. And if what I've planned to serve for a dinner party doesn't defrost in time, I don't run water over it or melt it down in the microwave, or wring my hands. I just put it back in the freezer and order pizza.

I guess a lot of people could point at me and say it's clear that my personality is slipping down. But going from an A to a C is not a tragedy to me. It seems like I'm having a lot more fun, and I even have the time to realize I'm having a lot more fun.

So this year, my New Years' Resolutions are to just keep on keeping on. Seems to me, that's a lot.

Blooms

I have witnessed some extraordinary changes in my lifetime, like when my Aunt Filene went cold turkey and quit smoking after thirty years. I was also there when my Great Uncle Bubba switched from R.C. to Pepsi and, in 1965, voted Republican after being a Democrat for sixty years. Change is not easy, at least in my mind.

Over the last five years now, I've been wanting to stop feeding my cats on top of the washing machine. They like it up there where they can eat in peace three feet above the dog, and I like it, too, since I can toss their empty cans right into the recycling bin, which is on top of the dryer. Yet every time I want to do a wash, I have to lift all of the cats' eating paraphernalia off the top of the machine so I can put my laundry in. It's an awkward system I've gotten myself in the middle of. But then, the only time I have found change easy is when I was thirteen and what my friends did had me switching from one thing to another about as fast as if I were xeroxing them.

Last week, though, my mother-in-law told me about how her dogwoods bloomed this year, and I am inspired. She had seven white dogwoods that each spring dotted her yard with their blooms. Three years ago someone gave her a pink dogwood for her birthday, and she planted it in the middle of the others. The next spring when the dogwoods bloomed, she had two pink trees and six white ones. This year she had three pink dogwoods and five white ones. There's not a good explanation for this.

People at the tree nursery say there's a chance this change might be explained by cross pollination. But no one is real certain. It's well known that if you plant field corn next to sweet corn, the sweet corn won't taste like it's supposed to. And a flower called Torenia can change from white to purple when planted beside the purple ones. To do this, though, it has to make it through the winter and last awhile. It's also known as the wishbone flower because if you push its blooms aside and look straight down into its works, it comes out of the soil in the exact shape of a chicken's wishbone.

I don't know if my mother-in-law's dogwoods have hidden desires to bloom pink, or if the plant named Torenia is secretly wishing to be a purple chicken. I prefer instead to think of their sudden changes as being rooted in magic, because I'm pretty certain that it's only magic that is going to get the cat food off the washing machine.

Mother's Day

I have a friend who lives at Cross Creek. She moved there over a decade ago from up North, and she would have left probably any number of times except that she fell in love with a man from the Creek. And that made all the difference. Apparently men at the Creek take the romancing of a woman very seriously.

For instance, a first date might be only a midnight fishing trip under a full moon on Orange Lake. It might be a frog gigging, or a beer shared out on a wooden bench near the Creek until it is dark and quiet, so that then you can listen to the alligators bellow in Lockloosa. And you'll know when the courting gets serious if a fella invites you to ride a boat out into the cypress woods after a big rain to watch the water run into the lake. But no matter if you are fishing, gigging, or watching water, it's a pretty sure fact that all the while, a certain magic is being practiced on you. So that afterward, it is very likely, your life will never be the same.

Creek men are aware of their power. And they strut it comfortably. For instance, it was reported that at the Marjorie Rawlings' house, the staff spotted a snake sneaking into one of the rooms, and out of desperation, called one of the Creek men. After all, a man who has grown up at the Creek knows more than you ever want to know about snakes and how to handle them. As the story goes, this Creek man sauntered up the steps to the house, saying he'd handle that snake, just point him to it. Then went into the room where the snake was and shut the door. In a few minutes he came back out and announced,

"That's a female chicken snake. And it won't take me but a minute to get her to move on out of here."

One of the caretakers was really curious and asked, "But how do you know it's a female snake?"

The creek man didn't even blink. "Because she quivered when she looked at me," he said.

I guess that really does say it all. Yes, the men at the Creek have a certain powerful charm. And it's said that everybody knows when a creek man is seriously courting a woman, because that's the only times he wears shoes.

So after my friend fell under the spell of one and married him, then stayed there to raise a family with him, she had to learn how to take on all sorts of new ways of thinking and saying things. When she became pregnant with their first child, she says she had to relearn how to announce that fact. For out at the Creek no one is ever pregnant. No. Rather it's that you're fixin' to have a youngin'. And then when the second one came, it was that she was fixin' to have another one. In fact, my friend says, since she has made her life at the Creek, she has found that almost everything she does has the word fixin' in it.

Last year on Mother's Day, she was in the kitchen fixin' to have a cup of tea when her husband sauntered up behind her, put his arms around her waist, and said to follow him, that he was fixin' to give her her Mother's Day present. He then led her outside, and on the way, grabbed his rifle, so that in only a minute they were standing under the giant magnolia that shades the whole side of the backyard. Then he propped his rifle on his shoulder and aimed it up toward the tree.

My friend says the blooms were like round white stars, perfuming the air with a sweetness that was like the smell of warm honey, or of spun sugar. Then her husband said to her, "Pick out one darlin'."

And when she raised her hand toward a bloom near the top, he focused his eye down the rifle's barrel and shot it down.

"Happy Mother's Day," he said, as he bent down and picked up the sweet white blossom that had fallen at her feet.

Spring Cleaning

I've been cleaning out my closets. I know that's what I'm supposed to do: get my life and closets in order, turn the kids' pads into dens and computer rooms.

From my own closet, I filled up a whole box with old clothes that I've been keeping for more years than I care to count. I considered them to be tests. Like the yellow velvet hot pants that date from 1969 which have been my measure for knowing when my figure would have fully recovered from childbirth. After twenty-three years, it is clearly time to give up the ghost on that. And the red dress that I wore to my cousin Betty's wedding in 1975 — it went in the box, too. For it will no longer hide the things I now want to hide.

I moved to the storeroom to sift through those boxes that, over the years, I had added to from the children's closets. I decided to part with the imitation leather vest and chaps that my son wore when he was four. Size wasn't a consideration for that, after all I could have saved them for grandchildren. But that idea seems so foreign and will exist so far in the future. And my son now is in college with dreams of cars and motorcycles and women. The thought of him as a cowboy has long been ridden out and put up. I threw in, too, the gangster suit that he had picked out, so long ago now.

I gave to the box the grown-up suit my daughter wore when she went to the legislature as a kid senator for a day. It would still fit, but her idea of a power suit has changed now, and anyway she could never accept wearing something she once wore in the tenth grade. The jacket fit me, though, and I thought long and hard about keeping that part of the power suit for myself. But if I wore it and one of her friends saw me in it and recognized it as the suit that had gone to the Capitol — well, my grandmother used to have a saying about that, that I might be seen to be trying to steal her thunder.

I taped up the box and put it in the trunk of my car and drove it down to a place that accepts and resells used clothes. Then I went on to washing windows and getting my taxes paid.

Yesterday I went down to the corner store for some more Windex. It was a really warm day, a day when summer slips in like a movie preview, and I saw walking into the door of the grocery store a young woman in yellow shorts that, I swear, were my 1969 hot pants. She was pulling along by the hand a little boy in cowboy chaps and a vest, and he had six-shooters strapped on and was doing a mean swagger. Those chaps sure looked like the ones my son had worn. But what I was real sure of was that the young woman at the check-out counter, right in front of me, was definitely dressed to the nines in my daughter's power suit.

It was all I could do to keep from running up to all of them and just blurting out, "Hey, that used to me mine," and "Just let me tell you where all those clothes have been!" But I didn't. Not only would it have seemed crazy, and sort of rude, but also it would have broken the spell.

It's rather wonderful, that sort of connection: seeing parts of my life on other people.

Daylight

Benjamin Franklin thought up the idea of Daylight Savings Time, but he didn't stick around long enough to know what it felt like to adjust to it. He thought it would be a grand idea if shops opened and closed earlier to save on the cost of whale oil and other stuff that made lamps light up back then.

Now that we are living with it, we have come up with some hints to remember what to do: fall back in the fall and spring forward in the spring. It's a whole hour we've put into motion here. I guess Benjamin Franklin was thinking about that saying, "The early bird gets the worm." But this year I've been having so much trouble springing forward that every morning when I've finally waked up enough to think, my first thought has been, "Oh just let the bird have the dern worm."

Actually, even though Benjamin Franklin thought up the idea of saving daylight, it didn't get put into practice until the First World War. It was signed into law by President Wilson on March 31, 1918. I guess everybody wanted a little extra time to fight after supper. But only a year later, as soon as the war was over, the law of Daylight Saving Time was repealed because no doubt all that fighting while springing forward had just worn everybody out. It was in 1974 during the energy crisis that we took the idea on for good.

Of course it's a whole lot easier in the fall to fall back an hour, but then I find myself arriving everywhere too early, and by nightfall all that waiting has pooped me out. The best thing about falling back, though, is that for a while in the middle of the day it feels that I have had two lunch hours. And for someone like me that is a real boon. For since I don't seem to be either a morning person or a night person, everybody expects a whole lot out of me at lunch.

It's the falling back that gives me an inferiority complex. If I admit that I don't plan to see the eleven o'clock news and have no hopes at all for *Saturday Night Live* for at least a couple of months, I feel like a nerd and an old person. And when I have to spring forward, it feels so unnatural that I envy puppies and even my own old dog now who sleeps just whenever she wants and doesn't fret about missing meetings or going to bed while it is still light. It seems to take me about a month of giving up ten minutes every day until I can comfortably live in the same daylight as everybody else, and then I like it.

My mother-in-law says that by the time we get into June, there'll be enough day left after supper to build a house. If I can make it to June, I guess I won't mind hearing my neighbors hammering and nailing an addition onto their house, or mowing their yard at 9 P.M.

The fact is, I grew up with this saying about how our football team was going to beat the daylights out of somebody else's football team, and that always put daylight into the plural form. You just never said you were going to beat the daylight out of someone, so clearly you had to save it up. As for me, though, I'd just as soon put it in motion, ten minutes at a time.

Packing

Well, we decided to move to a new house. I know I should have turned the kids' rooms into a guestroom and a computer pad. It just seemed so much easier to buy Skip a whole farm, then move him out to where it will be just him and me and.....?

But the day the moving company got involved, things took a wacky turn. The fact is, all these moving companies have a policy of letting people who are getting ready to move use boxes that have already moved someone else. Apparently these boxes just keep going and going, moving all these families' stuff from state to state, until their sides fall in — (not the families but the boxes) — and their tops sink and cave in onto themselves like my Aunt Filene's cheeks whenever she took her teeth out. So when you get the empty boxes delivered to you, they have some other family's name already written on them and then code words on where to put each one, like, "Chinese Chess Set, Yellow Study," or "French Copper Cookware, Kitchen."

When I started packing up my own household, I became really depressed. Everything I owned sounded so humdrum. Here I had lived in this one house for twelve years until both kids were gone and had started calling me by my first name. I had never had anything so exciting as French cookware or even a yellow study to put something like a Chinese chess set in. The sides of my boxes were labeled with pitiful codes like "pots and pans, put them just anywhere near the kitchen," and "sheets, set 'em beside any bed." It was when I picked up a box and saw written on it the words, "Wilson Family, Tudor Birdhouse, Put This In The Swimming Pool Cabana" — that something snapped in me. Forget the words Wilson and Cabana. I didn't know the Wilsons and never hope to. It wasn't personal, and I didn't give a hoot about their cabana. It was the idea of a Tudor birdhouse that got my killer instinct going. That's what's strange about a killer instinct, if you have one at all, because you never know what's going to bring it out, and then what it's going to do, once it's out.

The truth is that on many evenings, I've played hours of Bridge and Scrabble and Trivial Pursuit and never once felt a twinge of my killer instinct. I've gone home with scorecards from bowling that looked like I'd been drawing cartoons of bagels, and not once did I give a flip. So how in the world could something like packing up a household make me walk around the house spouting that I was going to pulverize them, kick their backsides, turn them into toast?

First, I labeled a box with the words Israeli Underwear, and then added the instructions, "Put it in the Master Bath."

Then I wrote on a box, "Semi-alive Ruby Skinned Python, Set It Down In The Family Room," and in parenthesis I added, "Be Careful, He Sleeps Only During The Day."

Next I labeled one of those great big wardrobe boxes that are big enough for someone to stand up in with the words, "Food for the Semi-alive Ruby Skinned Python."

All afternoon I just kept going, writing on every box the code words for mysterious and outrageous contents. I went from "Ultra-precious and Recently Cleaned Russian Jewels,"to just simply the label, "GREAT UNCLE BILL," with, "P.S., Please keep right side up."

When we got to our new house, and the movers had carried in and set down every one of my boxes, I looked at them — not the boxes but the movers. After all, these poor sweaty men were the only way I had to measure my score against the Wilsons and their Tudor Birdhouse. The movers were standing there exhausted, blurry eyed and speechless. Of course all afternoon they'd had to do a good bit of reading, and my handwriting isn't really all that good, but it was something else besides eyestrain and confusion that I was seeing in their faces.

For most of my life, I've been drawn to the power of fiction. And for one afternoon, I think I finally got to see the effect of my own, up close and personal.

Wild Turkeys

Last week I was washing my dishes at my new kitchen sink when I looked out my window and saw nine buzzards sitting on my pasture fence. They were lined up all in a row looking west. If they'd been looking straight into the kitchen window at me, I might have had to go hide in the barn, and even resort to a stiff swallow of Wild Turkey.

But after a closer look, I discovered they were wild turkeys. They couldn't be anything else. They were the size of buzzards, but they were the brown color of rained-on mud. They were sitting so still they were like wood and were sized like those Russian dolls where the not-so-big-one can fit into the big one, and so on down the line, until you have just one doll hiding all the rest inside.

The dog ran out of the house and barked, and the turkeys fluttered up a short way, then landed in the middle of the pasture and did a fast turkey walk, brisk as Olympic race walkers, into the piney woods.

Every day they came back. They sat on the fence and looked west, and I washed my dishes and looked north, out the window at them. They'd walk around in the pasture for a while, then go off and hide in the woods.

One of my neighbors told me that wild turkeys travel in flocks of nine, like a baseball team, minus the designated hitter. I thought this was such an intriguing idea, I drove into the little town fifteen miles from my house to ask around about where I could find an expert on turkeys. When I explained that I didn't mean cooking them or stuffing them, I was directed to a store that outfits hunters. That's where I met Wayne, a four-time Florida State Turkey Calling Champion, and this year, the Number One Turkey Caller in America. He is a young man, still in his twenties, with a mustache and a tall straight-up-all-the-way build. He was more than happy to fill me in on wild turkey society, and how one gets to be the best turkey caller around.

Turkeys are often seen traveling in flocks of nine, but that's not a hard and fast rule. Wayne taught me that there are four species of wild turkeys, and the one visiting at my house was the Oceola Turkey. They come in all sizes. The babies are called poults. Jennies are teen-aged hens, Jakes are the young turkey dudes, and the Old Gobblers are the ones who need only a hen to keep the population going.

It's the Old Gobblers that the hunters hunt. They are big turkeys with red faces and can make fans of their tails. A long beard comes out of the bottom of their necks, and a hunter is limited to killing only two of them in one season. According to Wayne, wild turkeys are smarter than anybody. They can see the sun glint off of a hunter's rifle quicker than a jet plane can streak by. That's why to hunt turkeys, you have to have a turkey caller with you, so as to bring the turkeys to you. And you have to be covered up in spotted camouflage gear, absolutely everywhere, even your watch and the gold in your teeth, if you have any.

Wayne sold me a Quaker Boy World Champion Beginner's Double Turkey Caller. The package says it's a win-win call with ease of use and great sound. I took it home and squatted down in the tall grass of the pasture. I put the caller in the roof of my mouth and pressed my tongue against it. Step four in the instructions says to say Chee-uck, and air will be forced between your tongue and the reed, and sooner or later a sound will develop into a yelp. But when I did all that, the only sound that came out of me was a buzz like a fly caught between the window screen and the glass.

I turned around to head back into the house. As I did, it seemed I could hear all of my wild turkey neighbors heading off in nine different directions. Talking turkey is a whole lot harder than it seems.

As yet, not one of them has come back.

Building the Ark

When El Niño hit us, I started thinking about the Ark. You know, El Niño, the thing that was out there in the Pacific Ocean like a floating hot plate. And the Ark, that great big boat in Genesis that Noah made when it rained for forty days and forty nights, so it was left up to him to save the Animal Kingdom — which included even his children and wife. Because never before in all the years that I had lived here had I seen so much rain!

Out at my farm, it rained for seven days and seven nights, and on the fifth day, I started getting nervous. I reread Genesis, not only to give me the dimensions and blueprints on how to build an ark, but maybe also to give me some hope that I wouldn't have to. I found out that it was the rainbow that God created to remind Him and Noah that never again would the earth be flooded out completely. But when I looked out of my window, there was no sign of a rainbow, and no sun even to make one. That's when I went to the grocery store.

I stocked up on cat food and dog food and bird food and horse food and cow food and dip and salsa for the New Year's Day Football games; then I looked around my garage to see what might be the makings of an ark. My husband's bass boat was all I'd have to work with. In Genesis, it's said that Noah's Ark was a three decker, and I'm sure I know why. With all those different kinds of animals in there, Noah had the potential for fireworks, so it only makes sense that he had a first class deck, and then a coach class, and poop deck. On any boat a poop deck means the stern, but on an ark, I'm sure it serves a whole different purpose. So I looked around my farm to see what I could use to make three different levels on our bass boat.

I found some old crates that oranges had come in, and some old boards where part of the fence had fallen down. I was ready to drag them all up to the garage and go to work. I'm not much with a hammer and a nail. I knew that when I finished it was going to be embarrassing, with me and my animal menagerie floating around as the El Niño representatives of Alachua County. In fact, when my husband and children got wind of my plan, they said they'd rather take their chances on land than on my ark.

On the morning of the seventh day, I was standing there all alone in the garage watching the rain still coming down in steady drips as if somewhere up there a water pipe had broken and no one could find a plumber. If I carried out my plan of getting on my home-made ark, I figured I'd have to put the cats in cages, Skip in a rain coat, my dog in galoshes, and...that's when it dawned on me. I'd be loading up a gelding, a spayed dog, three neutered cats, and me all by myself at an age — well, let's just say not likely to perform any bio-logical tricks that could get me on the cover of Time magazine.

I'm pretty sure that's why an hour later, the rain stopped, and the sun came out, and the waters began to recede. I kept looking for a rainbow, but I guess there was no need. I got the message: I'm not the right one to save the whole animal kingdom and mankind.

Birthday

Yesterday was my birthday, again. The only person I mentioned it to was my neighbor. What bothered me about it this time was that two weeks ago I put my nightgown on backwards and didn't notice until morning. I was ashamed about this for a while. But then, my neighbor doesn't seem to be embarrassed by any thing. He's a cowboy whose whole livelihood is tied up in cows. There must be something about that that, after a while, makes someone want to get close to people. In fact, after I moved here to our farm, for the first three months, every time I saw him, he'd ask me to marry him. That flustered me a bit. In fact, I didn't know what to say. And then finally I just told him the truth — that I already was.

"Well, I know that Darlin'," he replied. "But when I ast ya, don't it make ya feel good?"

Well, yes it does.

Now he hangs over the back fence and talks to me whenever I go out to feed Skip, which I have to admit, too, I often do in my nightgown. And I know what that leads you to think — but no, my nightgown didn't have anything to do with his marriage proposals. He has asked me to marry him while I was wearing overalls, manure-covered jeans, and raincoats that nearly touch the ground. And if I have talked to my neighbor more than once while I was wearing my nightgown backwards, he has never mentioned that, either. In my mind, he is a real gentleman. But I know, too, he has a philosophy to let people discover those sorts of things for themselves.

Anyway, when I confessed to him that I just couldn't believe I'd slept all night (well, I don't ever anymore sleep all night; it's about one or two times I have to get up now) and I had never once discovered that I had my nightgown on backwards, my neighbor said, "Ah heck, that ain't nothing. All the hair on my head's gone to other parts."

He went on to give me blow by blow details on how over the last year all the hair he's now growing seems to be coming out of holes or spreading across hills, like from his ears and nose and on the top of his shoulders and down his back. As for me, well, hair isn't so much of a problem as the fact that frequently now I've got jet lag. But I haven't been anywhere.

Every once in a while my neighbor and I ride horses together, too. And yesterday when we both got on — well, I use a ladder now — and he was about ready to swing up on his horse beside me, he said, "Don't mind me, I've just gotten a good bit noisy, lately." The snorting his mare made, while he sort of rock-climbed up the side of her, covered up whatever he was talking about. But then as we moved off down the road, I realized that what I thought were our saddles squeaking was really my neighbor's knee.

All morning we rode side-by-side, looking over the landscape and his cows while talking about everything and nothing. I told him that the day before I had discovered some part of my refrigerator had fallen off, and for the life of me I couldn't decide where it was supposed to go.

"Oh, lots of things are like that," he said. "Could be that part's just for looks. I bet the refrigerator works just fine without it, don't it?"

I agreed that it did. Then when we turned our horses around and started back home, I saw on the roadway from where we had just come a great clump of hair. Of course, we both knew that it could have come from his mare. But then, too, well...but neither of us wanted to stop to examine it. We just rode on past in silence.

And then, "Happy Birthday," he said.

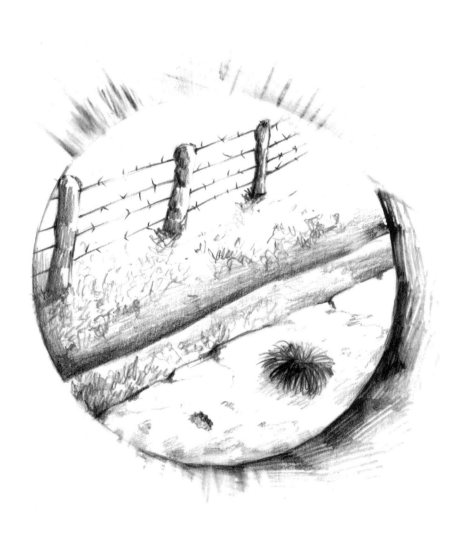

Fly Swatter

I am in love with my fly swatter, and I hardly know a thing about it. For days, I've been trying to come up with something about its background. I've looked up fly swatter in the dictionary, and in the encyclopedia, and I even looked it up on the world wide web. But everything comes back nada, no dice, zip, zilch, and a goose egg. No one is even given credit for inventing it. It doesn't appear in the encyclopedia. And the dictionary gives it only one line. It cuts it into two words, too. Fly and then Swatter. It is defined as a swatter used to kill flies. If my kid wrote that down on an English theme, he'd get an F; I know because I helped him write three themes, and on the first two we got an F; so I now know how his teachers think.

Actually my fly swatter and I didn't come together quickly. It was a matter of finding out a need for each other. It started when I got the grand idea to build a farm house in the middle of a cow pasture where I could build a place for my horse Skip in the back of the garage. I fenced out the cows only a short distance from the front yard so there wouldn't be much grass to mow. And so I have the cows on one side and Skip on the other, and about a week after I moved in, I discovered I was surrounded by flies.

Now killing a fly's not anything that really bothers me, but I don't tend to do it until the fly just nearly pesters the ever lovin' life outta me, and then that's it. I grab whatever is handy. The first few months in my new house, I went after flies with rolled up newspapers and the tips of towels and the straw end of a broom. And once I even popped one on the head with a cast iron skillet. He was a quick devil, though, and I didn't get the best of him until I'd smashed a light bulb and cracked the tile on the counter around the stove. That's when I decided to get something that is meant for this one deed and nothing else. That's when I went to the hardware store and asked for the big enchilada, the kitchen bazooka, the hired gun that I could hide in the cabinet under the sink. "I want a fly swatter," I told the man behind the counter.

"Aisle two," he said and pointed.

His nonchalance was proof enough that what was to become the love of my life was already being unappreciated. For as soon as I walked down aisle two, the man behind the counter left his cash register to help some woman pick out needle-nosed pliers. For crying out loud! Now I ask you, what's so hard about picking out needle-nosed pliers? But then when I got to where the fly swatters were hanging, I saw why I was sent there alone. There just wasn't anything but one kind, one color, one shape to trot out. White wire handle, blue plaster swat head. And that was it. It was even less than a dollar. Only 79 cents.

I took it home and hung it under the sink. And then one afternoon I left out a watermelon rind and a crack in the front door, too. A few hours later a couple of dozen flies were taking a house tour. It was pretty exciting to pull out the big enchilada and go to work. Now you see, the thing about my fly swatter is that the white wire handle lets its big blue plastic head swat forward with a zap. It can swat a fly faster than you can say spaghetti, and a whole lot faster than you can spell spaghetti. And when you let it go, you can really get a charge. I mean it's a whole lot better than scream therapy, or water therapy, or coming one number short of winning the lottery. It's a bigger blast than playing Pac Man or any of those other silly video games.

That's what I want in the dictionary. That's what I want on the World Wide Web, too. I want it to say, Fly Swatter—the neatest little invention since the can opener. Or better yet, the can itself. Better even than the old dictionary. Better even than sliced bread and.... Oh well, I'll stop. Just don't ever ask to borrow my fly swatter. Nope. You have to get your own.

Zucchini

Our garden is coming in, and I am neck high in tomatoes. Thank goodness there are a lot of things you can do with tomatoes. Sliced with a little mayonnaise on top is not shabby. And then of course, there's spaghetti, and pizza topping, and tomato relish, and so on into tomato oblivion.

And thank goodness, too, this year I've wised up and didn't plant so much as one zucchini.

I'll admit the reason I got into trouble years ago with zucchini is that I have no green thumb whatsoever. And the zucchini plant doesn't give a fig what color a thumb is. It'll grow in sand, pitch black shade, a crack in the pavement, or even my garden. It's the most desperate vegetable I know. In fact, it's the nerd vegetable in anybody's dirt.

I'm sure that it's because nobody really likes it that it grows so prolifically. I knew a man once who was hospitalized for chronic insomnia because he believed his zucchini vines couldn't wait to crawl over his house and latch onto him and smother him in his sleep.

The only thing I know that is charming about zucchini is its name. Zucchini. Zucchini. Zucchini. It's really a blast to say. It can also be a deterrent for delinquent behavior. For instance, I used to threaten my children with sending them to school with an all zucchini lunch. Zucchini bread sandwiches. And zucchini cake, and zucchini muffins, and lord-help-us plain zucchini strips. Nobody wants to sit next to anybody who has zucchini in his lunch box.

I also think the best thing about zucchini is that if you can remember how to spell it you can raise your self-esteem. I just wish in some of these runoffs for the national spelling bee they would use the word zucchini to weed out about a couple of hundred smug spellers.

The only dish with zucchini in it that I have ever found that was even half way delicious was zucchini and tomatoes cooked until neither one of them resembled themselves. In fact, this is how I got into growing tomatoes in the first place. I needed something to go with all my zucchini.

Let's face it. Zucchini was put on earth to make us feel good. I know a man who has a two-foot zucchini stuffed and mounted in plastic sitting on his coffee table.

Growing something big is nice to point to. And we can also feel real smart when we can declare with absolute certainty that we'll never hear anyone on their death bed cry out for zucchini. Or request it on death row as their last meal.

But darn, now that I've said all this about zucchini, I'm starting to feel a little sorry for it.

I hope all my past experiences with zucchini haven't made me crazy. I'd hate to think that I could actually find myself tomorrow morning watering my tomatoes and wishing for a little taste of zucchini. But then, I don't guess it's ever too late to plant zucchini.

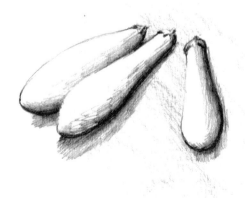

Sweat

Sweat is something I grew up being taught not to talk about. Girls didn't sweat; we glowed. Back then, too, we heard on the radio a song called *Cry Me a River*, which always gave me the hee-bee-jee-bees thinking about all that water coming out of someone's eyes. But now in my twentieth summer in Florida, I'm sure I've sweated at least a river. I'm not a bit ashamed of it, either. I accept the fact that it's going to take me about three sets of clothes to get through a day, and I've vowed not to cry Uncle and run into some air conditioning more than once an hour, either.

I'm well armed, though. I have sweat bands and sweat suits and fluid replacement drinks. Sweating is something my body was designed to do, I know. It's when I don't sweat that I should worry.

That's why I'm keeping a close watch on my dog's tongue. It's the only thing she has to sweat with. She can hang it out now to just about her knees, and she doesn't mind, either, if it slips over to one side and flops on her shoulder. At about noon, she rolls onto her back and sticks all four legs up. It seems she is asleep, but her tongue is going thaaa, thaaa against her teeth like a little red ticket that someone is pushing out from a teller's booth. Her nose now takes up the slack, puffing air in the rhythm of, *The Little Engine That Could*. If her tongue gets this sort of rest, I figure she'll make it through the summer.

I still don't know why, though, people are so reluctant to talk about sweat. Or why we've been brought up to answer any question about whether or not something is bothering us by saying, "No Sweat." In the dictionary it says that to sweat means to exude in droplets, as moisture from certain cheeses or sap from a tree. It means to release moisture, as hay in the swath. Or to ferment, as tobacco during curing. It's like that old song, *Birds do it; Bees do it*, but then in that song, sweat isn't what they are talking about.

If there were a song about sweat, though, it could have in it something to the effect that cheeses do it, trees do it, hay does it in the swath, and tobacco, too. I had to look up the word swath, and it means that the hay sweats in the path where it has just been cut. I think I know what that feels like.

But knowing our culture, no one would ever be brave enough to sing about their sweat. No doubt if some country western singer did, he'd just moan a good long while about his broken heart and how his true love had died or taken him to divorce court and to the cleaners, too. And then he'd end up with some chorus about how the experience hadn't bothered him a bit, not really.

And if he made a video? Well, I don't have a doubt in the world but that we'd get to see him sitting on his truck hood strumming his guitar with his hat tilted back and singing, "No sweat," over and over, clearly denying what we see dripping off his nose.

Mildew Days

The time between mid-July and September is known as Dog Days because the star named Sirius, which in Latin means Dog Star, rises and sets with the sun during this time. But here in Florida, what I know rises and sets with the sun, and then goes on creeping and spreading all through the night, is mildew.

It creeps in somewhat like the fog into Chicago that the poet Carl Sandburg described as coming in on little cat's feet, except that my mildew picks and chooses where it will descend and then lies down and rolls like a dog onto something that smells dead.

It camps in the shower, settling into the cracks with no shame and coats the shower curtain like a shadow that someone accidentally left behind. It is the ghost of summer trying to hang on and screaming bloody murder when I pull out the bleach.

In the middle of August, it gets serious and puts on combat gear, camouflaging itself as gray dust under the flaps of my saddle and as hard black freckles on my white horse's legs. It burrows down into the thick coat on my dog's back with an unrelenting itch, and I know I am in trouble when it occurs to me that even now my dog has mildewed.

Overall, I have a pretty mild disposition, and I have a hard time seeing that a lot of fights are worth fighting. But the onslaught of mildew turns me ugly. I get out a mean wire brush that could blister the hide off a rhinoceros. And I squirt bleach onto everything that will stand still. I hire power washers and cleaning services and turn up the air conditioner. I aim my hair dryer at things that don't even have hair. My only hope is to keep everything dry until the humidity goes into hibernation.

Of course all this tuckers me out by late September, which is the time I think should really be named Dog Days. Because it's only then that I get to flop down on a lounger out by the pool and lie like a dog.

Organized

This year I've made a promise to myself — I swear I'm going to get organized. I got shamed into wanting to do it, and shame is about the only thing that really gets to me. It gets me off the couch to take out the garbage, since it's a shame to let the garbage men stop at my house and have nothing for them. It makes me clean my horse's feet before the farrier comes, and wash my hair before I go to the hairdresser. It puts me up to buying raffle tickets for things that I don't give a hill of beans about, since otherwise I would get looked at by all these big pitiful-looking eyes that would accuse me of not caring. It seems I walk around my house hearing voices saying, "Tend to me. Tend to me. Tend to me." The last call I got was from my purse.

Now, as we all know, purses are mysterious things, and I won't go into the emotional symbolism they can carry (that's a whole different story that I'll get to next). But what they carry in terms of helping a woman get through an ordinary day is staggering. Frankly, I couldn't do my income tax or order a pizza without the information my purse holds. It's more of a filing cabinet than a purse. But then, the importance of my purse is inherited. My Aunt Filene said she carried everything in hers from an unloaded 38 to the kitchen sink and parts of her first husband (which parts, she never would say). She even slept with her purse and never, under any circumstances what-soever, let it out of her sight, which is what she said she should have done with her first husband.

What got me so ashamed of my purse was the day I checked out of the grocery store in line behind a woman who had a purse the size of a cow's patoot. "Wow!" I thought, you could be lost in there for days. But much to my shame, she pulled one of those organizing books out of it and wrote a check for her groceries, double checked the bill with a calculator, displayed her check cashing card, and any other card you would ever want to see, cleanly secured in its own plastic window. Near the top part of that purse I also caught a glimpse of all of the tools you would ever need for an on-the-spot manicure and an oil change, as well as a coupon book that was probably hold-ing a couple of million dollars worth of clipped money-saving deals. That was as far as I got to look, since it was now my turn to pay for my own groceries, and I had to come up with my own checkbook from the bottom of my own purse, as well as a pen and some form of identification that didn't have a wad of chewed gum sticking to it. I never did find a pen.

When I got home, I started thinking about Benjamin Franklin. It seemed to me he'd once had a deep desire to get organized too, so I looked up his autobiography to see how he'd handled it. I found out that actually he was after moral perfection, which contained thirteen virtues, of which orderliness was only one. After a good long while of hacking away at each virtue, he admitted that attaining order was the only one that really brought him to his knees.

He compared it to the story of a farmer who took an ax to a blacksmith with the request to make the whole ax as gleaming as its edge. The blacksmith made the farmer turn the grinding wheel while he held the ax against it, and after a good long while of this awful work, the farmer had a revelation. "I think I like a speckled ax best," he said.

Benjamin Franklin always told this story when he explained that he'd decided it was best to leave himself a good bit disorganized, since otherwise if his character was so gleaming in all respects, his neighbors would, no doubt, envy and hate him.

I think I like the idea of a speckled ax, too. In fact, if I fall short of getting organized, I'm going to quote Benjamin Franklin and learn to live with my shame. Heck! he didn't even have a purse.

Purses

There is something that goes on between a woman and her purse that no one on this earth can explain. It is mysterious and beyond comprehension, and it taps into a primitive, unchartered part of the brain.

Personally, the only way I could come close to explaining how a woman chooses her purse would be to talk about things like cell mitosis, and the forces of biological osmosis, or why Julia Roberts married Lyle Lovett.

For instance, suppose you see two women of equal size and shape — in fact they are twins — walking down the crowded center aisle of a mall, and they are both clutching their purses close to their bosoms, and yet the purses themselves are nothing alike. One is a rectangle made out of black suede with outside zippers and inside pockets, and the other one is an oval stitched out of leather with outside snaps and a buckle strap that fastens its top on like the skin of a drum. Yep, these women know something which not even physical torture could make them talk about.

If you ask them how they chose their purses, they would say something about this little snap or that little pocket, and then, well, there was just something about its shape.

But the truth is, what we women don't like to talk about is that when we do go shopping for a new purse, we are actually waiting for the right one to call out to us. That's why we have to spend a couple of hours in a lot of different purse sections in department stores leaning slightly forward over a rack of purses, touching this one lightly, turning that one over, actually picking up another one and rooting around in its insides. Occasionally a few of us will even lean forward and take a sniff. We move on to rack after rack, or to a bin where they are displayed in piles which we can actually almost climb into and dig around. Nothing makes a woman happier.

When I was raising my daughter, it took her quite a while before she learned the language of purses. And then when she hit high school, she changed from one purse to another about every three months, moving to another style or brand or handle length. After all, she was just beginning her education.

One Saturday when we went out on a purse hunt, we found ourselves standing in our seventh purse section of a department store, sweaty and wrinkled and hungry. By then I was slumped over a counter on my last leg, and still she was moving from one rack of purses to another, looking confused and dazed.

Finally I took her by the shoulders, stood her in the middle of the purse section so that all of them were encircling us like a wagon train, and I coached her, "It's here. I know it's here. The right one for you is somewhere very close. Just listen."

Now, some people might say it was the bedraggled look on my face, and the hang-dog hunch of my shoulders that made her head straight for a little rust suede job with an outside zipper. But we all know the truth, and I didn't discuss with her exactly what that purse said. That is always a private matter just between a woman and her purse.

I also know that somebody could bring up the fact that Mr. Freud wrote all kinds of things about the symbolism of purses and what they mean to women. But if that's the truth, couldn't ole Siegfried

also have written a fancy paper about how men choose their wallets
— bi-fold or triple-fold — and the variation of how those wallets feel
in a back pocket?

No, I think the truth lies in more mysterious realms. I don't
think, either, it's a bit unreasonable for a woman to fight to the death
with anybody who wants to snatch her purse. Or at the least, cry out,
if a robber does get the best of her, "Oh, all right. Go ahead. Take my
money, just leave me my purse."

WD-40

I have time now to do things that a fine upstanding mother wouldn't admit to. Like wander. Or get lost on purpose. And yesterday I got lost on a street in a distant part of town. So I just pulled over, parked, and walked down it until I came to a hardware store.

It was one of those old stores, the kind that has a wooden floor that is uneven and worn, so that when I walked between the aisles I heard myself crackling and squeaking. I sounded like trees blowing in wind.

Behind the counter were three men who were having a fine time visiting. There were just two other people in the store shopping, and I was the only woman. One of the men was telling the clerk about some tool that had refused to work. He said he'd had trouble with it from the get-go. Get-go was the perfect way to describe a beginning, I thought, and I dillydallied behind a display of iron cookware so that I might be close enough to hear more.

They were now talking about childraising, and one after the other launched into telling a story about some outrageous mischief that one of their children had gotten into, like driving off in the family car when they couldn't see over the steering wheel, or leaving on a faucet and flooding the living room, or setting the backyard on fire. Whenever the height of the story came, the father who was telling it would let loose with a guffaw that seemed to me like a mixture made up of a dash of exasperation along with chunks of admiration and affection. The story always ended with the father resorting to what he described as "fanning someone's backside" or "curing a ham for good."

I looked up over the shelf of cast iron Dutch ovens that were shoulder high on me and saw a display of pulleys and something called shrimp tubing. When I started down the aisle with all the plumbing fixtures on it, I was amazed at how many of them were named after the parts of the human body. Female joints and male joints. And my every footstep was telling everyone in the store exactly where I was.

Up near the ceiling at the back door was a sign that said "Shoplifters will be beaten and stomped. Survivors will be prosecuted." I didn't doubt it, but I hadn't planned to steal anything anyway. It certainly defined the spirit of the place though — independent, blunt, old-timey, yet quick to get to the point.

I hung out for a while with the chains, fascinated with the yards and yards of them on rollers, each with links in different sizes, and I tried to imagine all the different dogs and swings that could be held by them.

Suddenly behind me I heard and felt the weight of someone on the same floor boards where I was standing. When I turned around, I saw one of the men who had been behind the counter. "Can I help you?" he asked.

I know I looked stupid, just wandering around the store as though I had no idea of what I was there for. In any other store, especially in a woman's clothing department, I would have said very quickly, and without thought, "Oh, I'm just looking." But here — just looking in a hardware store? I doubted that would fly.

Flustered, I glanced to my right. My eye caught a display of bright cans on a shelf. "Oh, here it is," I exclaimed and walked to it. "I came in for a little of this." I held up a small spray can of WD-40. "And isn't this nice," I said. "It's purse size."

"Darn tootin'," he said, which seemed just right for him to say.

When I followed him up to the cash register and paid for it, he didn't offer me a paper bag to put it in, either. I didn't really expect him to. I just opened up my purse and he dropped in my can of WD-40, then rushed from behind the counter to hold the door open for me.

Do you suppose in his world, every woman he knows is packing her own personal can of WD-40?

As I walked back down the street and got in my car, all I know is, it sure did make me feel complete.

Potato Gun

My life has been suddenly, totally, and irreversibly changed. I have shot a potato gun.

It all happened the night of the Super Bowl when a lot of friends came over to watch it on our big screen TV, which we have because neither my husband nor I want to admit we need glasses. Having a big screen TV is like reading those books in super big print. But anyway, my good friend Dave brought along something even better and bigger than a big screen TV. He brought along his potato gun.

It was right when the Super Bowl was about to get under way that he called me out onto the porch of my house and asked, "You wanna shoot it?"

"Not right off hand," I thought. I've never liked guns — hate the whole idea of shooting and war and everything that goes with it. But then, Dave picked up the long solid white contraption of his potato gun and started teaching me how he'd made it. It has the barrel of a PVC pipe, probably about the size of the one that is hooked up to my septic tank. And at the base there is a joint in it, which in plumber's terms, is probably called an elbow. And in the elbow Dave had put one of those little red buttons like the one that starts the fire in a gas grill.

Well, after I saw how it was all made, Dave looked at me and held out the potato gun and said, "Now you know you want to shoot it."

I'll admit I was a little intrigued, but mainly I just didn't want to hurt Dave's feelings. He seemed so all-out dedicated to and excited about his potato gun. So I said, "Yeah, well, let me have a crack at it."

It was then that something started happening that I never thought could ever happen. For Dave reached down into a sack of potatoes, pulled out a fat Irish one, stuffed it into the PVC barrel so that part of its skin was peeled away by the pipe like a curly fry that then fell onto the porch floor. Next he picked up a can of hair spray and sprayed it down the barrel behind the potato. Then he handed me the whole gun.

"Hold tight," he said, "because it's got a pretty good kick."

"Yeah, yeah, yeah," I thought, sort of tickled by the thought of how many ways I knew to cook a potato, and that maybe this was going to be best one.

I aimed out over the back pasture, and I pointed up toward the top of the trees. It was getting dusk, and peach-colored streaks of the sunset were still visible over to my left. From inside the house on the Super Bowl Warm-up I could hear that it was getting close to time for the kickoff. Pretty soon Cher would be coming on to sing the National Anthem. And that was something I did not want to miss. For Cher and I are nearly the same age, and I wanted to compare how our body parts were holding up.

Quickly I propped the potato gun on my shoulder and held my aim steady and then pushed the little red button. Sure enough, the hair-spray explosion kicked me back a few steps. But in front of me, I began to behold a sight no less wonderful than my fifty-year-old memories of turning cartwheels in cool summer grass. For the most gorgeous Irish potato-in-flight that I have ever seen arced up over the trees and went longer than the whole length of a football field out across the pasture, then touched down a few feet from our pond. Meanwhile inside, Cher was letting loose with the opening phrase of the Star Spangled Banner. So I put the potato gun down and hurried in to hear her sing the rest.

I don't know, maybe it was the sight of Cher singing about rockets flaring red and bombs bursting in air. Or maybe it was the feel of my own inner child waking up and kicking around inside of me. But anyway, I ran back out to the porch and asked Dave if he'd let me shoot his potato gun again.

Don't tell anyone, though, because Dave also told me that when Lawton Childs shot one over the governor's mansion, the police drove over real quick and told him he couldn't ever do that again.

But heck, I've never had such a good Super Bowl.

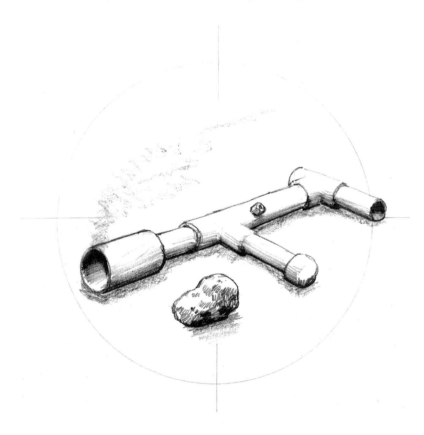

A Day's Work

We used to have a standing joke in my house. In the early morning, when we could barely hold our eyes open and my husband and I were sucking our first cups of coffee, he would say to me, "What are you going to do today?"

I usually had a list. And it went like this. "First, I'm going to get the scum out from under that little chrome rim around the sink. I'm going to do about four loads of wash, then change the sheets, wash the dog, find the cap to the milk which I have a sneaking suspicion is somewhere under the couch, help man a booth at the kids' school at a fundraiser, vacuum the house, and write a novel."

Actually before I got to number one, I had to wait for the house to clear. Which meant that the kids got off to school, my husband went to work, and the washing machine repairman had come and gone and taken his grease and wrenches with him. Then I could get down to business.

As for the scum, I went at it with a butcher knife with a little Comet on the blade. I stuck it up under the edge of that chrome rim around the sink and slid it while it made a slicing noise that curled my toes. Meanwhile I was running back and forth to the washing machine changing loads. The dryer hummed like my grandfather used to snore, but then there were three loose nickels in it and a pair of tennis shoes, and my grandfather had a mean deviated septum that made his whole brain sound loose.

When I pulled out the first load from the dryer to fold it, one of the pairs of my son's soccer shorts had lost that little rope that goes through the tube-like waistband to hold them up. I found it stuck in with a bunch of towels. So I got a great big safety pin, tied it to the rope and started scooting it through the waistband by using my fingers to feel through the cloth. When I had worked it nearly to the end, I used my teeth to get a good grip on the pin head, and I pulled the rope on through. I folded up the shorts, really proud of what I'd done.

The dog hair on the sofa was harder to deal with. I had to resort to adhesive tape to get it all off. Then I sprayed the couch with Chanel Number Five to get rid of the smell of dog and for at least one night, the dog. For she doesn't like the scent of Chanel Number Five and is loath to sleep anywhere near it.

I found the top to the milk in the leaves of a houseplant. By the time I was supposed to man that booth at the school fundraiser, I had all four loads of laundry stacked on the kitchen table. The floors were vacuumed, and there was no smell of scum or dog. The whole place looked like a picture in a magazine.

I went to the school for the fundraiser. I picked up the kids, and we stopped at the library on the way home. When we walked in, the dog jumped off the bed to come meet us. The kids knocked their laundry piles off the table when they set down their books. My husband tracked in grease from where the washing machine repairman had parked his leaky truck. I accidentally spilled gravy by the sink, and it flowed all up under that rim. When my son reached down to give the dog a hug, that drawstring waistband on his shorts gave out, and since he was handcuffed by his soccer britches at the ankles, he fell against the stove, hit his knee, and bled all over the kitchen floor.

That night as I lay in bed, I went over my list. I know this sounds strange, but I felt certain that I'd had a religious experience. For I'm sure I understand how God must have felt after He made the world, and then stepped back and watched Man walk in.

Dr. Dolittle

I have always wondered who in the heck Dr. Dolittle was. All the time I was reading that children's book about him to my children, I kept thinking, "Wow, this is a really strange man." I just couldn't quite understand what it was all about — this person who talked to animals, who had a special, unusual beast called a Pushmi-Pullyu with a head on both ends ready to go in opposite directions. And yet my kids loved that book. And I loved reading it to them. So here we went, almost every afternoon, over and over and over, dawdling through the pages with Dr. Dolittle chatting away to a whole slew of critters.

But now that my children are gone, I have come to know Dr. Dolittle. And he is me.

Here I am left in this big old house with all the pets my kids grew up with, and I am talking their ears off as if we are all on Oprah. And as for that Pushmi-Pullyu, well I met him, too. But it was a couple of years back when both my kids were teenagers, and we were scratching off and slamming on the brakes at the same time in our relationship a lot. Most of the time I pushed and they pulled, and yet being so tightly related, we didn't have the choice to come apart.

But now here my husband and I sit at the dinner table with all this leftover parenting sort of talk. Sooner or later he'll ask me what the cat did today, and I'll tell him and add that I'm really worried about how she'll eat nothing but chicken livers. Or we'll laugh at the dog because she barks in double time, since she can't hear so well anymore and is hell bent on staying scary.

The strangest thing about how I'm talking to these animals is that when I had my children, I never talked baby talk to them. It wasn't in my nature, for some reason or other. But now I find myself leaning over the dog and talking sweet nothings in sounds that could pass for a chicken clucking or a squeeze toy being mashed. Don't ask me why.

And thank heavens, the dog won't tell.

Names

It has occurred to me that it is strange indeed that we should go through a whole life with only one name. What got me to thinking about this was when I recently went to the mountains to the same place where I'd gone on vacation when my children were small. Back then my daughter was ten, and she and I rented horses at a stable and rode up a trail in the mountains to look at the waterfalls and to feel the cool air that our summer doesn't allow.

This time, when I went, it was fifteen years later. So it was just I, alone, who decided to go back to the same stable and ride up the mountain trail once again. A big red horse was assigned to me. She was twenty-four years old, I was told; and her name was Lula Belle. But as I climbed up on her, I suddenly realized, she was the same horse I had ridden up the mountain fifteen years before. Only back then, she'd been called Hurricane.

D. H. Lawrence said that having one name is as bad as having only one jacket and one hat. It is like having only one relation, only one blood relative in the whole wide world. He advised parents to never set a child afloat on the flat sea of life with only one sail to catch the wind.

I have to admit, I took to a different sail when I was in the second grade and decided to rename myself Ann. I insisted that everyone call me that. And I signed all my school papers with Ann in the top right hand corner, just as my teacher instructed us to do. But it took her a couple of days to figure out that there was not a new girl in the room, and that I had not dropped out of the second grade.

This teacher and I didn't always get along. She didn't like the fact that I could already write script and read the newspaper, because my older brother had taught me how. But on this name thing, she was more than good. She said, "All right, Ann." And for the next two days accepted me as just that.

But then, during the second week of my name change, she started calling me Shelley Ann. And when I insisted that I wanted it the other way around, that I wanted the Ann part to come first, she said, "Honey, I'm too old to start learning who everybody is all over again."

It seems to me though, now that I am getting older, I am changing the names of other people whether or not they want me to. Because the names I learned years ago are not always the names I put with faces now. In fact, living in the same place for twenty years has put a lot of words in my address book. And if I don't see a person for many months or even several years, his or her name can allude me as surely as trying to catch hold of wet soap.

It works the other way, too. I've been at places and at parties where my name has been changed by people who haven't seen me in a pretty long while. To tell you the truth, I'm never offended — except maybe once when I was called Malvernia.

But even so, when I go to holiday parties this year, if I am introduced by a name I have never before been called, and if I speak to someone by a name they have never before heard, I think we should just consider taking them on. After all, Lula Belle was still Hurricane. And I am still Ann. And just as Shakespeare once wrote about a rose, that it by any other name, would still smell as sweet, I figure that if that can go for a bush, it can just as well go for us.

True Love

Lately I've been looking for signs of true love. Considering that in Washington a whole slew of men in pin stripe suits have been standing up and publicly admitting they've had the hots for somebody they shouldn't have at one time or another — and they're real sorry for it — I've been looking for signs of true love in all the most unusual places. And lo-and-behold if I didn't just recently find it at the cosmetics counter at Dillards.

It was two days before Christmas, and I was standing there trying to decide on some perfume for my mother, when this John Wayne type fellow walked up and parked himself beside me. He had gray hair and was way over six feet tall with a chest big enough to spread a flap jacket wide. In a voice as gravelly and deep as a concrete mixer, he asked the clerk about some skin conditioning system his wife had read about in some magazine.

"Oh, yes," the clerk said, "We have a One-Two-Three- Step skin care that is wonderful. And to top it off, we have a Turn Around Cream that works miracles."

This man shifted his weight from one foot to the other and let out a bull-sized sigh: "Dadgum it," he said. "I hate being here. It's worse than walking around with an ingrown toenail. And now I've got to stand here and make all these decisions. It's downright humiliating." Then he turned to me. "What would you do?" he asked.

"I'd go for the miracle," I said. But you could tell he didn't like my advice, probably because he'd asked for it.

He shifted back and forth from his right foot to his left and then looked at the clerk and ordered, "Well, give me the One -Two-Three," he said. "But if she wants to turn around, she's going to have to come back and do that for herself. I'm pressed for time, and I'm not in the mood."

While the clerk went off to get his order, he turned to me again and said, "And now this afternoon I've got all six of my children and their children coming in. Fourteen grandchildren and all their noise. Doggone it! I now regret being so damn fertile."

"Umhumm," I said, and thought he was fitting all my ideas of a typical grumpy old man. He was probably about like John Wayne after the fifth day of a cattle drive when he'd forgotten his Preparation H.

After the clerk brought him his skin care system wrapped up in a red bow, he sighed again, pulled out his credit card, and eventually sauntered off. Meanwhile, I stopped spraying all the sample perfumes all over me and decided on one to give to my mother.

A week after Christmas, the perfume I had chosen had broken my mother out, so I was standing once again at the cosmetics counter in Dillards. I was dotting the i in my name on the credit card slip, when I felt something at my back. And there was my grumpy old John Wayne putting a bear-sized paw on my shoulder.

"You were right," he said. "It was the galdern Turn Around Cream she was most interested in all along. And now here I am right back here to get it."

I stepped aside and let him move in close to the counter. He raised his hand to motion to the clerk, and as I walked off, I glanced back. If this wasn't a sign of true love that I'd just witnessed, I don't know what is.

Goodness

Now that I have lived over half a century, I find that new things are catching my attention. I can remember being more than just a little bit fascinated with the dark side. In college I studied wars in history classes; I took abnormal psychology three different times. Of course two of them were disguised by other names in the psychology department. But they were still about deviance and aberrations, which mostly amount to learning about what human beings are capable of doing to each other. In fact, thinking about Hitler and Al Capone and Lizzie Borden could hold my attention the same way my children used to watch Mr. Rodgers peel a carrot.

I learned last week, though, that I am branching out. I was talking to a young man who had seen a movie about mobsters and about how one of them had taken his daughter to college, and while he was getting her settled, he took a break and went out and killed someone. He came back, checked his daughter into her dorm, and went about making sure her life there would be safe and worthwhile. The young moviegoer was fascinated with how this evil existed in what was otherwise a normal lifestyle.

I guess this moviegoer was probably about twenty-five, and he was so enthusiastic over the film he had seen, I didn't have the heart to tell him that I have lived long enough to have seen that plot in at least three other movies, and two books to boot. Evil has always been a big seller. You can bet on it every time and come in first in any entertainment poll.

But what I was thinking about while I was listening to this movie being described was not how fascinating evil can be, but how fascinating it is to learn how some people can stay good their whole lives. George Orwell said that on the whole, human beings want to be good, but not too good, and not quite all the time. Harry Truman put behind his desk the quote by Mark Twain that reminds us to always do right — this will gratify some and astonish the rest.

On the flip side of this, Thoreau said that if he knew for a certainty that a man was coming to his house with the conscious design of doing him good, he would run for his life.

Well, I agree there is nothing worse than a do-gooder, goody-two-shoes, who in other words could be called a busy body with improvement on his mind. Now, I don't know if you know, but I know — at least after having raised two children I can say I know — that if any idea for improvement is ever going to take place, it can't come from the person who needs improving. No. It's got to be planted, so the person who gets improved thinks it was his idea all along.

So how is it that a person could be good through a whole life? I don't mean that a person doesn't make mistakes. But how is it that one could live a whole life and never lose hope, or the ability to love, or the desire to be loyal? To not take constant pot shots at fellow human beings, or to treat the earth like a home with only a thirty-year mortgage?

Some days, it seems to me that goodness is as scarce as hen's teeth. Then at other times, well... whenever I see it now, however seldom and in whatever place, and no matter how boring it might seem to someone else, I stop, lean close and turn it around and around in my mind. I like to keep it there for a while, twirling like the tiny colored pieces of glass in a kaleidoscope. Yep, by the time you're my age, goodness is a never-ending fascination.

Shelved

When my daughter was six, I was thirty-six. And it was my job, I thought, to teach her about the basic American character. I took her to a state fair. I wanted her to see all those pigs and cows and jams in jars, and the quilts that many women's hands had sewn.

She pulled me instead to the carnival rides. And as we walked by, a man who looked like B.O. Plenty in the cartoons of my childhood leaned out from one of those wooden milk bottle booths and held out a baseball. "Come on, little girl," he said, "how about a try? Three throws for half a dollar, and you might win you a prize."

Behind him were all these stuffed animals sitting on shelves like a choir.

"Can I have fifty cents?" my daughter asked me.

"It's not a good idea," I told her.

"Why not?" she asked.

"It's a waste of money," I said.

"Why?" she asked again.

"Look," I said, "nobody ever wins at those things." I went on and told her the unwatered-down truth about how I'd spent my whole childhood and tons of money throwing baseballs at wooden bottles, or else picking up some wooden duck out of a stream of water to look for a magic number on his bottom. And I never won anything. Or at least the most I ever got was a cheap little diamond ring that left my finger green.

"Then loan me fifty cents from my allowance," she said.

I couldn't believe I'd given birth to such a hard-headed gambler. Nothing I could do would distract her. Finally, an hour later, I gave her the loan. In fact, I was prepared to let her borrow her allowance for the next seventeen years. It wasn't going to be pretty, but I was willing to stand by and watch her sling baseball after baseball at those dumb milk bottles, until she had little league elbow and was begging me for mercy.

The B.O. Plenty look-alike handed her the first baseball and grinned at me. All right, so she did look cute. But I was getting even. He might be taking us for a quick ride, but I was teaching her about life.

The first baseball whizzed by and hit the canvas backstop with a thud. B.O. Plenty grinned again and put our money in his pocket.

The second baseball went wild, and old B.O. had to duck. Then I grinned.

On the last throw, my daughter reared back and let the baseball go, and it hit the bottle on top of the three bottle pyramid, and that was it. She was clapping and laughing as if she'd dunked all three.

"What do I get, what do I get?" she kept yelling.

B.O. Plenty handed her a sausage-shaped dog. It was ugly and tacky. But my daughter didn't care. She walked over to me and held it up next to my face. "See," she said. "You don't know everything."

She is a grown woman now. And when she packed up to move into a place of her own, she left me that ugly little carnival dog sitting on her dresser in her room. I have it now on a shelf in my new kitchen.

Every once in a while I look up at it. And every other week or so, I carefully dust around it. It's faded and a little bit torn, and still the ugliest little dog I hope ever to see, but it solidly sits there, carefully reminding me that her life is very much her own.

Gone

I have stumbled over a new and exciting truth. With the children gone, there is no one to embarrass. I can take the garbage out in my fuzzy house shoes. I can spit and cuss and have a Coke for breakfast and eat my supper on my lap in front of the TV without worrying about ruining anybody's character who might be looking up to me.

My dog looks up to me, but she's mostly interested in what I'm putting in my mouth. And just in case I might be ruining her, I've taught her to wait politely until I have the first bites of whatever I'm into, and then we share the rest. (She can even take little bites of a pork chop off a fork now.) She doesn't say a thing, either, when I don't comb my hair and just stick it under a baseball cap, or when I walk around all day in my riding boots with the spurs still attached. I've gotten all sorts of comments from men at filling stations who pull up in their Doulies — those double-tired trucks with four doors — while I am pumping gas. They look down at my spurs and say I am their kind of woman.

I think what is happening is that my rural southern roots are popping out like the roots on a blonde who for years has dyed her hair, so now no more color will take. I am who I was soon after I was starting out: not exactly childless but yet without a child under my feet. It is I who now is playful and likely to stop in the grocery store and work the gum machine. Back in Arkansas, we had a word for people who acted somewhat like me. "They were gone," we said, "just totally and irretrievably gone." It carried the connotation of crazy, but it also meant that whoever was gone had gone happy, too.

So I've decided to keep going, and last month I bought myself a truck. It is a big candy apple red pick-up that matches my red neck that seems to be rising up with no shame. The only shame I have is that I can't quite get the hang of using this truck. I have yet to park it between any two white lines in town. And the vacuum cleaner that I put in the back to take to get repaired — it rolled all around, then tipped over on a U-turn and fell out onto the street.

For one whole day I made my dog ride in the back, where I know dogs such as she are supposed to be. But when we drove through Burger King to get our Whoppers, she terrorized the people who were trying to hand them to me. Then in the middle of town on one of the busiest streets, she jumped out to run after a cat, which meant that we nearly caused three separate wrecks. And that surely would have landed us on the six o'clock news.

At first, when I brought the groceries home, I put them in the back, too. But by the time I reached the driveway, the sacks had all turned over, so the cans and fruit had rolled into the corners as though my truck bed were a pool table. Getting the hang of using this truck is going to take awhile, I've decided. And until then, I'm just going to put my dog and my groceries and my vacuum cleaner in the front with me.

Today I was stopped at a red light and happened to look over at the car beside me, and in the front seat was the best friend of one of my kids. He was someone who had practically grown up in my house, had even, at times, called me "Mom."

I turned down the radio and tapped on my truck window. I waved and called out his name. But he only glanced my way. So when the light changed, I scratched off and pulled around him, and the dog hung her head out the window and let her tongue trail.

I knew he wasn't acknowledging us because he didn't want to. Or was embarrassed to. No. It's just a new place in life for all of us. And I know I have to be patient.

It always takes a good little while now to recognize me.